Peter Buchan

Gleanings of Scarce Old Ballads

With explanatory notes

Peter Buchan

Gleanings of Scarce Old Ballads
With explanatory notes

ISBN/EAN: 9783744796712

Printed in Europe, USA, Canada, Australia, Japan

Cover: Foto ©Thomas Meinert / pixelio.de

More available books at **www.hansebooks.com**

SCARCE
OLD BALLADS

Gleanings

OF

Scarce Old Ballads

WITH

Explanatory Notes

BY

PETER BUCHAN

ABERDEEN: D. WYLLIE & SON
PETERHEAD: D. SCOTT
1891

DAVID SCOTT
PRINTER AND LITHOGRAPHER
PETERHEAD

GLEANINGS

OF

SCOTCH, ENGLISH, AND IRISH,

SCARCE

OLD BALLADS,

CHIEFLY

Tragical and Historical;

Many of them connected with the localities of Aberdeenshire, and to be found in no other collection extant.

WITH

EXPLANATORY NOTES,

BY

PETER BUCHAN.

"On the lear'd days of Gawn Dunkell;
Our country then a tale cou'd tell,
Europe had nane mair snack and snell
    At verse or prose;
Our kings, were poets too themsell,
    Bauld and jocose."

Peterhead:
Printed by P. Buchan, and Sold by
LEWIS SMITH, Aberdeen; A. SANGSTER, and G. MUDIE, Peterhead; A. & J. WILSON, Banff; G. MAITLAND, Elgin; W. & D. LAING, and J. DICK & Co. Edinburgh; & W. SUTHERLAND, LONDON.
1825.

TO

SIR WALTER SCOTT, BART.

THE

FOLLOWING GLEANINGS

OF

ANCIENT SONG

ARE

Dedicated,

With every Veneration *and* Respect,

BY

His most Obedient Servant,

THE EDITOR.

PREFACE.

The mind of the man of taste seems to be absorbed with attention when he enters a picture gallery, or exhibition of historical paintings.—What the paintings are to the connoisseur or amateur in this divine art, Ballads are to the historian and lover of literature. Sir Joshua Reynolds says, the pictures displayed on the walls of a room, are the thoughts of the artists; and, as family pictures are much esteemed for their representing to us the face and countenance of our ancestors, and bringing to our recollection the favoured features of those who are now no more! those things that pourtray the mind and soul ought to be more dear to us. The ancient Ballads of Caledonia are venerated by those lovers of their country who delight in the native imagery of their homes, and in hearing the martial and warlike deeds of their forefathers said or sung in the enchanting voice of their fair countrywomen.

There is a noble sublimity, a hear-melting tenderness, (says an emminent author,) in some of our ancient Ballads, which shew them to be the work of a masterly hand: and it has often given me many a heart-ache to reflect, that such glorious old bards—bards, who very probably owed all their talents to native genius, yet have described the exploits of heroes, the pangs of disappointment, and the meltings of love, with such fine strokes of nature,—that their very names (O how mortifying to a bard's vanity!) are now buried among the wreck of things which were.

PREFACE.

The few that are here presented to the public, are not given upon an account of their poetical merit, although several of them have stood the test of ages, but as pictures of the mind, wherein is to be seen in panoramic view, the heroic deeds of other years, the loves, the joys the hopes, the fears, the crosses and enjoyments that dispirited and animated the lives and generous actions of those who once brandished the broad swoard in defence of their rights as men, and proved their bravery as heroes.

I have also added a few original pieces from my own unworthy pen, not at the request of any officious friend, nor to expose my own folly as a follower of the muses, but that the volume, small as it is, may be as generally pleasing as possible to those readers who do not pict themselves on their attachment to every antiquated scrape, nor adepts in antiquarian lore. Critics may cavil, and show their ill-founded sarcasms in venting their spleen upon them, merely because they have not been *smoked* in some old woman's wardrobe for the last hundred years; but this is a fault will be dailing lessening—for what they are not just now they soon will be!

The Explanatory Notes are not such as I would have wished them, for being much hurried at the time they were written, I was limited to a few days to finish the whole, and even then much interrupted; so that any one never so little conversant with subjects of the kind, may judge of the difficulties I had to encounter, but I plead no excuse—the world admits of none. However, I have endeavoured to make them as correct as possible, i.e. regarding their cronological order. The reader will easily perceive I have used many obsolute words and

PREFACE.

phrases, now altogether exploded from the classic page of the refined modern. This I did not do for the sake of appearing pedantic, but that there might be some similarity between the ballads and notes.— The critic will also perceive, they are not critical, but explanatory; and that a few grammatical and typographical errors have inadvertantly escaped my notice till now, when it is too late to correct them.

Should my countrymen, and those of taste, give encouragement to the present attempt to rescue from the devouring fangs of oblivion, many of the thoughts that emanated, in the sweet cadence of poetic numbers, from many of their forefathers who now lie cold in the clay, which they once held dear, though now nearly annihilated, I have some hundreds beside the present, which have not made their appearance in any formidable shape these several centuries: if not, they shall be consigned to moulder away in sullen silence in some solitary cell, unheard of and unknown.

PETER BUCHAN.

Peterhead,
October 1825.

CONTENTS.

	Pages. Ballads.	Notes.
Sir James the Rose, (old way,) ...	9	185
Sir James the Rose, (modern way,)	11	ib.
Alcanzor and Zaida, ...	18	186
The Lake of the dismal Swamp, ...	22	ib.
Bryan and Pereene, ...	24	187
Young Gregor's Ghost, ...	26	ib.
The Jew's Daughter, ...	33	188
Cruel Lammikin, ...	35	ib.
The Faithless Captain, ...	40	ib.
The Gosport Tragedy, ...	46	189
Rosanna's Overthrow, ...	51	ib.
Fair Rosamond, ...	59	190
The Death of Leith-Hall, ...	66	191
The Baron of Braikley, ...	68	ib.
The Earl of Aboyne, ...	71	192
Loch-in-var, ...	74	193
Queen Eleanor's Confession, ...	77	ib.
The Savage Blackamoor, ...	80	194
Lord Thomas and fair Eleanor, ...	86	ib.
Lady Anne, ...	90	195
The Bonny Earl of Murray, ...	91	ib.
Clerk Colvil and the Mermaid, ...	92	ib.
Sir Patrick Spens, ...	94	196
Andrew Lammie, ...	98	197
The Northern Lord and Cruel Jew,	105	ib.
Mary's Dream, (old way,)	112	198
Willie Wallace, ...	114	199
James Francis Edward Keith, ...	117	ib.
Lorenzo, ...	120	ib.
The Death of Ella, ...	121	200
Lord John, ...	122	ib.
Lord Thomas of Winsberry, ...	127	ib.
Maria; or, the Maniac's Song, ...	129	201

CONTENTS.

	Ballads.	Notes.
Mary's Death,	130	201
Summer,	131	ib.
Winter,	132	ib.
Beautiful Sue,	133	ib.
May Morning,	135	202
Roseate May,	136	ib.
Cheerfu' Nancy,	137	ib.
Edwin,	138	ib.
Spotless Peggy,	139	ib.
My Mary,	140	ib.
Love,	141	ib.
Enjoyment,	142	ib.
Generosity,	143	ib.
Ingratitude,	144	ib.
Poverty,	144	ib.
The Complaint,	145	ib.
The Storm,	146	ib.
The Sherriff-muir, Amazons,	147	ib.
My Mantle,	149	203
Mossie and his Mare,	151	ib.
The Cadgers o' Whitecrook,	153	ib.
The Pipers o' Buchan,	154	204
Lord and Lady Errol,	158	205
Lord Salton and Auchanachie,	161	ib.
Bonny John Seton,	161	206
Mary Hamilton,	164	ib.
The Burning of Frendraught House,	165	ib.
Frennet Hall,	169	209
Lady Keith's Consolation,	171	210
Nae Dominies for me, Laddie,	172	ib.
Logie o' Buchan,	175	211
By the side of a Country kirk wall,	176	215
Charly now that's o'er the sea,	178	216
Adam o' Gordon,	180	ib.

GLEANINGS OF TRAGICAL BALLADS.

Sir James the Rose,

(OLD WAY.)

O HEARD ye o' Sir James the Rose,
    The young heir o' Buleighan ?
For he has kill'd a gallant squire,
    Whase friends are out to tak him.
Now he has gane to the house o' Mar,
    Whar nane might seek to find him ;
To see his dear he did repair,
    Weining she would befriend him.

Whar ar ye gaing, Sir James, she said,
    O whar awa are ye riding ?
I maun be bound to a foreign land,
    And now I'm under hiding.
Whar sall I gae, whar sall I rin,
    Whar sall I rin to lay me ?
For I hae kill'd a gallant squire,
    And his friends seek to slay me.

O gae ye down to yon laigh house,
    I sall pay there your lawing ;
And as I am your leman true,
    I'll meet you at the dawing.
He turn'd him right and round about
    And rowd him in his brechan :
And laid him down to tak a sleip,
    In the lawlands o' Buleighan.

He was nae well gane out o' sight,
    Nor was he past Milstrethen,
Whan four and twenty belted knights
    Cam riding owr the Leathen.
O hae ye seen Sir James the Rose,
    The young heir o' Buleighan?
For he has kill'd a gallant squire,
    And we are sent to tak him.

Yes I hae seen Sir James, she said,
    He past by here on Monday;
Gin the steed be swift that he rides on,
    He's past the Hichts o' Lundie.
But as wi' speid they rade awa,
    She loudly cry'd behind them;
Gin ye'll gie me a worthy meid,
    I'll tell ye whar to find him.

O tell fair maid, and, on our band,
    Ye'se get his purse and brechan.
He's in the bank aboon the mill,
    In the lawlands o' Buleighan.
Than out and spak Sir John the Graham,
    Wha had the charge a keiping,
It's ne'er be said, my stalwart feres,
    We kill'd him whan a sleiping.

They seized his braid sword and his targe,
    And closely him surrounded:
O pardon! mercy! gentlemen,
    He then fu loudly sounded.
Sic as ye gae sic ye sall hae,
    Nae grace we shaw to thee can.
Donald, my man, wait till I fa,
    An ye sall hae my brechan;

Ye'll get my purse thouch fou o' gowd,
    To tak me to Loch Lagan.

Syne they tuke out his bleeding heart,
    And set it on a spier;
Then tuke it to the house o' Mar,
    And shawd it to his deir.
We could nae gie Sir James's purse,
    We could nae gie his brechan,
But ye sall hae his bleeding heart,
    Bot an his bleeding tartan.

Sir James the Rose, O for thy sake
    My heart is now a breaking,
Curs'd be the day, I wrocht thy wae,
    Thou brave heir o' Buleighan!
Then up she raise, and furth she gaes;
    An in that hour o' tein,
She wandered to the dowie glen,
    An never mair was sein.

Sir James the Rose,

(MODERN WAY.)

Of all the Scottish northern chiefs
    Of high and warlike name,
The bravest was Sir James the Rose,
    A knight of meikle fame.
His growth was like the tufted fir,
    That crowns the mountain's brow;
And waving o'er his shoulders broad,
    His locks of yellow flew.

The chieftian of the brave clan Rose,
　　A firm undaunted band ;
Five hundred warriors drew their swords
　　Beneath his high command.
In bloody fight thrice had he stood,
　　Against the English keen ;
E'er two and twenty op'ning springs
　　This blooming youth had seen.

The fair Matilda dear he lov'd,
　　A maid of beauty rare ;
Even Marg'ret on the Scottish throne,
　　Was never half so fair.
Lang had he woo'd, lang she refus'd,
　　Wi' seeming scorn and pride ;
Yet aft her eyes confess'd the love,
　　Her fearful words deny'd.

At last she bless'd his well-tried faith,
　　Allow'd his tender claim ;
She vow'd to him her virgin heart,
　　And own'd an equal flame.
Her father, Buchan's cruel lord,
　　Their passion disapprov'd,
And bade her wed Sir John the Græme,
　　And leave the youth she loved.

Ae night they met, as they were wont,
　　Deep in a shady wood,
Where on a bank, beside the burn,
　　A blooming saugh-tree stood.
Conceal'd among the under-wood,
　　The crafty Donald lay,
The brother of Sir John the Græme,
　　To hear what they would say.

When thus the maid began :—My sire
  Your passion disapproves,
And bids me wed Sir John the Græme:
  So here must end our loves.
My father's will must be obey'd,
  Nought boots me to withstand :
Some fairer maid in beauty's bloom
  Must bless thee wi' her hand.

Matilda soon shall be forgot,
  And from thy mind defac'd :
But may that happiness be thine
  Which I can never taste.
What do I hear ? is this thy vow ?
  Sir James the Rose replied ;
And will Matilda wed the Græme,
  Though sworn to be my bride ?

His sword shall sooner pierce my heart
  Than reave me of thy charms.
Then clasp'd her to his beating breast,
  Fast lock'd into his arms.
I spake to try thy love, she said :
  I'll ne'er wed man but thee ;
My grave shall be my bridal bed,
  E'er Græme my husband be.

Take then, dear youth, this faithful kiss,
  In witness of my troth ;
And every plague become my lot
  That day I break my oath !
They parted thus : the sun was set :
  Up hasty Donald flies ;
Come turn thee, turn thee, beardless youth,
  He loud insulting cries.

Soon turn'd about the fearless chief,
    And soon his sword he drew ;
For Donald's blade before his breast,
    Had pierc'd his tartans through.
This for my brother's slighted love,
    His wrongs sit on my arm.
Three paces back, the youth retir'd,
    And sav'd himself frae harm.

Returning swift, his hand he rear'd
    Frae Donald's head above.
And through the brain and crashing bones,
    His sharp-edg'd weapon drove.
He stagg'ring reel'd ; then tumbled down
    A lump of breathless clay ;
So fall my foes, quo' valiant Rose,
    And stately strode away.

Through the Green-wood he quickly hied
    Unto Lord Buchan's hall ;
And at Matilda's window stood,
    And thus began to call,—
Art thou asleep, Matilda dear ?
    Awake, my love, awake :
Thy luckless lover on thee calls,
    A long farewell to take.

For I have slain fierce Donald Græme ;
    His blood is on my sword ;
And distant are my faithful men,
    Nor can assist their lord.
To Sky I'll now direct my way,
    Where my brave brothers bide,
And raise the valiant of the Isles
    To combat on my side.

O do not so the maid replies ;
    With me till morning stay ;
For dark and dreary is the night,
    And dangerous is the way.
All night I'll watch thee in the park ;
    My faithful page I'll send,
To run and raise the Rose's clan,
    Their master to defend.

Beneath a bush he laid him down,
    And wrapp'd him in his plaid,
While trembling for her lover's fate
    At distance stood the maid.
Swift ran the page o'er hill and dale,
    Till in a lonely glen
He met the furious Sir John the Graeme,
    With twenty of his men.

Where goest thou, little page ? he said,
    So late, who didst thou send ?
I go to raise the Rose's clan,
    Their master to defend :
For he hath slain fierce Donald Graeme ;
    His blood is on his sword ;
And far, far distant are his men,
    That should assist their lord.

And has he slain my brother dear ?
    The furious Graeme replies.
Dishonour blast my name, but he
    By me e'er morning dies !
Tell me where is Sir James the Rose ?
    I will thee well reward.
He sleeps into lord Buchan's park ;
    Matilda is his guard.

They spurr'd their steeds in furious mood,
    And scour'd along the lee ;
They reach'd Lord Buchan's lofty tow'rs
    By dawning of the day.
Matilda stood without the gate ;
    To whom thus Græme did say,
Saw you Sir James the Rose last night ?
    Or did he pass this way ?

Last day at noon, Matilda said,
    Sir James the Rose pass'd by :
He furious prick'd his sweaty steed,
    And onwards fast did hye :
By this time he's at Edinburgh town
    If man and horse hold good.—
Your page then lied who said he was
    Now sleeping in the wood.

She wrung her hands and tore her hair,
    Brave Rose thou art betray'd,
And ruin'd by those means, she cried,
    From whence I hop'd thine aid.
By this the valiant knight awak'd,
    The virgin's shrieks he heard ;
And up he rose and drew his sword,
    When the fierce band appear'd.

Your sword last night my brother slew ;
    His blood yet dims its shine :
But e'er the rising of the sun,
    Your blood shall shine on mine.
You word it well, the chief replied,
    But deeds approve the man ;
Set by your men, and hand to hand,
    We'll try what valour can.

Oft boasting hides a coward's heart;
   My weighty sword you fear,
Which shone in front in Flowden-field,
   When you kept in the rear.
With dauntless step he forward strode,
   And dar'd him to the fight :
Then Græme gave back and fear'd his arm,
   For well he knew its might.

Four of his men, the bravest four,
   Sunk down beneath his sword :
But still he scorned the poor revenge,
   And fought their haughty lord.
Behind him basely came the Græme,
   And wound him in the side :
Out spouting came the purple gore,
   And all his tartans dyed.

But yet his sword ne'er quate the grip,
   Nor dropt he to the ground,
Till thro' his en'my's heart his steel
   Had forc'd a mortal wound.
Græme, like a tree with wind o'erthrown,
   Fell breathless on the clay ;
And down beside him sunk the Rose,
   Who faint and dying lay.

The said Matilda saw him fall :
   O spare his life ! she cried ;
Lord Buchan's daughter begs his life ;
   Let her not be denied.
Her well-known voice the hero heard :
   He rais'd his death clos'd eyes,
And fixed them on the weeping maid,
   And weakly thus replies :—

In vain Matilda begs the life
    By death's arrest denied :
My race is run—adieu, my love—
    Then clos'd his eyes, and died.
The sword yet warm from his left side
    With frantic hand she drew :
I come, Sir James the Rose, she cried,
    I come to follow you !

She lean'd the hilt against the ground,
    And bar'd her snowy breast ;
Then fell upon her lover's sword,
    And sunk to endless rest.

Alcanzor and Zaida,

(*A MOORISH BALLAD.*)

SOFTLY blow the evening breezes,
    Softly falls the dews of night ;
Yonder walks the Moor Alcanzor,
    Shunning every glare of light.

In yon place lives fair Zaida,
    Whom he loves with flame so pure :
Lovliest she of Moorish ladies ;
    He a young and noble Moor.

Waiting for the appointed minute,
    Oft he paces to and fro :
Stopping now, now moving forwards,
    Sometimes quick, and sometimes slow.

Hope and fear alternate seize him,
  Oft he sighs with heart-felt care.—
See, fond youth to yonder window
  Softly steps the timorous fair.

Lovely seems the moon's fair lustre
  To the lost benighted swain,
When all silvery bright she rises,
  Gilding mountain, grove, and plain.

Lovely seems the sun's full glory,
  To the fainting seaman's eyes,
When some horrid storm dispersing,
  O'er the wave his radience flies.

But a thousand times more lovely
  To her longing lover's sight,
Steals half-seen the beauteous maiden
  Through the glimmerings of the night.

Tip-toe stands the anxious lover,
  Whispering forth a gentle sigh:
Alla keep thee, lovely lady;
  Tell me, am I doom'd to die?

Is it true, the dreadful story,
  Which thy damsel tells my page,
That, seduc'd by sordid riches,
  Thou wilt sell thy bloom to age?

An old lord from Antiquera
  Thy stern father brings along;
But canst thou, inconstant Zaida,
  Thus consent my love to wrong?

If 'tis true, now plainly tell me,
    Nor thus trifle with my woes;
Hide not then from me the secret,
    Which the world so clearly knows.

Deeply sigh'd the conscious maiden,
    While the pearly tears descend
Ah! my lord, too true the story;
    Here our tender loves must end.

Our fond friendship is discover'd,
    Well are known our mutual vows;
All my friends are full of fury,
    Storms of passion shake the house.

Threats, reproaches, fears surround me;
    My stern father breaks my heart;
Alla knows how dear it cost me,
    Generous youth, from thee to part.

Ancient wounds of hostile fury
    Long have rent our house and thine;
Why then did thy shining merit
    Win this tender heart of mine?

Well thou knowest how dear I lov'd thee,
    Spite of all their hateful pride,
Tho' I fear'd my haughty father
    Ne'er would let me be thy bride.

Well thou knowest what cruel chidings
    Oft I've from my mother borne,
What I've suffer'd here to meet thee
    Still at eve and early morn.

I no longer may resist them;
  All, to force my hand combine;
And to-morrow to thy rival
  This weak frame I must resign.

Yet think not thy faithful Zaida
  Can survive so great a wrong;
Well my breaking heart assures me
  That my woes will not be long.

Farewel then, my dear Alcanzor!
  Farewel too my life with thee!
Take this scarf, a parting token;
  When thou wear'st it think on me.

Soon lov'd youth, some worthier maiden
  Shall reward thy generous truth;
Sometimes tell her how thy Zaida
  Died for thee in prime of youth.

To him, all amaz'd, confounded,
  Thus she did her woes impart:
Deep he sigh'd, then cried, O Zaida,
  Do not, do not break my heart.

Canst thou think I thus will leave thee?
  Canst thou hold my love so small?
No! a thousand times I'll perish!—
  My curst rival too shall fall.

Canst thou, wilt thou, yield thus to them?
  O break forth, and fly to me!
This fond heart shall bleed to save thee,
  These fond arms shall shelter thee.

'Tis in vain, in vain, Aleanzor,
    Spies surround me, bars secure :
Scarce I steal this last dear moment,
    While my damsel keeps the door.

Hark, I hear my father storming!
    Hark, I hear my mother chide!
I must go : farewel for ever!
    Gracious Alla be thy guide!

The Lake of the Dismal Swamp,

(AN AMERICAN BALLAD.)

They made her a grave too cold and damp
    For a soul so warm and true;
And she's gone to the Lake of the dismal Swamp,
Where, all night long, by a fire-fly lamp,
    She paddles her white canoe.

And her fire-fly lamp I soon shall see,
    And her paddle I soon shall hear;
Long and loving our life shall be,
And I'll hide the maid in a cypress tree,
    When the footstep of death is near!

Away to the Dismal Swamp he speeds—
    His path was rugged and sore,
Through tangled juniper beds of reeds,
Through many a fen where the serpent feeds,
    And man ne'er trod before!

And when on earth he sunk to sleep,
    If slumber his eye-lids knew,
He lay, where the deadly vines do weep
Their venomous tears—and nightly steep
    The flesh with blistering dew!

And near him the she-wolf stirr'd the brake,
    And the rattle-snake breath'd in his ear,
Till he starting cried—from his dream awake—
Oh! when shall I see the dusky Lake,
    And the white canoe of my dear?

He saw the Lake—and a meteor bright,
    Quick o'er its surface play'd—
Welcome, he said, my dear one's light!
And the dim shore echoed for many a night,
    The name of the death cold maid!

Till he form'd a boat of the birchen bark,
    Which carried him off from the shore;
Far he followed the meteor spark:
The winds were high, and the clouds were dark,
    And the boat return'd no more.

But oft, from the Indian hunter's camp,
    This lover and maid so true
Are seen at the hour of midnight damp,
To cross the Lake by a fire-fly lamp,
    And paddle their white canoe!

Bryan and Pereene,

(*A WEST-INDIAN BALLAD.*)

The north-east wind did briskly blow,
    The ship was safely moor'd,
Young Bryan thought the boat's crew slow,
    And so leapt overboard.

Pereene, the pride of Indian dames,
    His heart long held in thrall,
And whoso his impatience blames,
    I wot ne'er lov'd at all.

A long long year, one month and day,
    He dwelt on English land,
Nor once in thought or deed would stray,
    Tho' ladies sought his hand.

For Bryan he was tall and strong,
    Right blythsome roll'd his een,
Sweet was his voice whene'er he sung,
    He scarce had twenty seen.

But who the countless charms can draw
    That grac'd his mistress true?
Such charms the old world seldom saw,
    Nor oft I ween the new.

Her raven hair plays round her neck,
    Like tendrils of the vine;
Her cheeks red dewy rose-buds deck,
    Her eyes like diamonds shine.

Soon as his well-known ship she spied,
    She cast her weeds away,
And to the palmy shore she hied,
    All in her best array.

In sea-green silk so neatly clad,
    She there impatient stood;
The crew with wonder saw the lad
    Repell the foaming flood.

Her hands a handkerchief displayed,
    Which he at parting gave:
Well pleas'd the token he survey'd,
    And manlier beat the wave,

Her fair companions one and all
    Rejoicing crowd the strand;
For now her lover swam in call,
    And almost touch'd the land.

Then thro' the white surf did she haste,
    To clasp her lovely swain;
When ah! a shark bit through his waist:
    His heart's blood dy'd the main!

He shriek'd! his half sprang from the wave,
    Streaming with purple gore,
And soon it found a living grave,
    And ah! was seen no more.

Now haste, now haste, ye maids, I pray,
    Fetch water from the spring;
She falls, she swoons, she dies away,
    And soon her knell they ring.

Now each May-morning round her tomb
    Ye fair, fresh flowerets strew,
So may your lovers scape his doom,
    Her hapless fate scape you!

Young Gregor's Ghost.

PART I.

Come all you young lovers in Scotland draw near,
Unto this sad story which now ye shall hear,
Concerning two lovers that liv'd in the North,
Among the high mountains that stand beyond Forth.

The maid was a daughter of a gentleman,
In the name of M'Farlane, and of the same clan:
But Gregor was born in a Highland Isle,
And by blood relation her cousin we style.

But where riches are wanting, we oftentimes see
Few men are esteemed for their pedigree,
His father was forc'd when he was a child,
To leave this realm,—for he was exil'd.

His lands they were forfeit, as I let you know,
Because of rebellion, the truth for to show;
Bread, gold, and vast riches, he with him did give,
For his education, and how he might live.

And solely he to the care of his friend,
Was left by his father for to be maintain'd,
He learn'd him indeed for to read and to write.
In the rules of arithmetic he made him profite.

In Latin and French he taught him also,
That he through the world was fit for to go,
The king then recruiting, all hands did employ,
While her father as a servant did use this young boy.

In all kinds of drudgery he made him to serve,
And still so he kept him as a corpse of reserve,
Such a beautiful young man was not in the place,
None could compare with him in stature and grace.

This charming Miss Katty was oft in the way;
One day, in love's passion, she to him did say,—
My dear cousin Gregor, I've something to tell,
Which now from my bosom this day I'll reveal.

You know that with courtiers I'm plagu'd to the
But you are the object that makes me to smart, (heart
If you can but love me, dear cousin, said she,
I'm happy for ever, and therefore be free.

Then said he, dear Katty, I'm all in a stun,
I suppose your intentions are nothing but fun,
For had I a subject to balance with you,
I'd count myself happy, your suit I might rue.

O! said she, dear Gregor, I'm no way in jest,
And if you deny me then death's my request;
You know the substance and wealth that I have,
'Tis enough to uphold us all gallant and brave.

I know that my parents for more riches are bent,
But a few years by nature will make them extinct;
To you my dear Gregor, I do make this vow,
That I never will marry another but you.

C 2

O then he consented, and flew to her arms,
And said my dear Katty, I'm kill'd with your charms
But if your parents this fond love should know,
They soon will carve out my sad overthrow.

Of that, my dear Gregor, be silent I pray,
This night we will part, and meet the next day,
Under the broad oak, by the cave in the glen,
Where more of my mind unto you I'll explain.

PART II.

Her mother next morning by the blink of her ee,
Perceived great love 'tween her and Gregor to be,
And she to her husband the same has reveal'd,
Giving orders to watch them as they're in the field.

All day then her father went walking about,
And after her still he did keep a look out,
Till hard in the evening, she went to the glen,
Where Gregor was waiting to hear her explain—

The way they would manage, and make matters go,
Her father did follow and heard her also,
He stepped in softly, stood over the cave,
And hearing the whole how they should behave—

At last he advanced, cried Gregor, what now,
Is this the reward from such an orphan as you?
You know I've maintained you since seven years old,
And now your intentions they seem very bold.

Then Gregor ask'd pardon, and this he did say,
Sir, I'm at your disposel, then do as you may,
The old man in a passion there chiding did stand,
Till Katty took courage and then speech in hand.

What mean you, dear father, on us for to to frown,
Was Gregor a beggar, I'm sure he's our own;
He's of our own kindred, our flesh and our blood,
And you very well know his behaviour is good.

'Tis him that I choose for a husband and shall,
Go give all your riches to whom that you will:
Do not think I'm a horse or a hog to be sold
Away to some numskul for nothing but gold.

The father in a rage to the mother did go,
And told the proceedings with sorrow and woe,
Yet seem'd as his anger that night had been gone,
Lest that young Gregor the place should abscon.

But he sent a message into Inverness,
Which brought out a party young Gregor to press,
And for to make ready no time gave we hear,
He ask'd but one favour, a word of his dear;

Which being denied him, the old man in a frown,
Said, soldiers can have sweethearts in every town;
At this the young lady cried out bitterly,
May the heavens requite you for your cruelty.

Young Gregor took courage and marched away;
When his captain view'd him this to him did say—
For the lady that lov'd you, I pity her case,
Who's lost such a beauty and sweet blooming face.

His lady cried out, what a wretch can he be,
Caus'd press this young man for no injury,
His long yellow hair to his haunches hang down,
O'er his broad shoulders, from ear to ear round.

Now Gregor considering his pitiful case,
Received the bounty and swore to the peace,
His captain unto him a furlough he gave,
To see his dear Katty once more he did crave.

Two lines he sent to her by a solid hand,
That he under the oaktree at midnight would stand,
For to wait upon her and hear her complaint,
And there for to meet him she was well content.

Her vows she renew'd with tears not a few,
And a gold ring on his finger as a token she threw,
Which was not to move, come death or come life,
Till that happy moment he made her his wife.

She fain would go with him, but he answered, No:
Your parents would follow and cause us more woe,
May the heavens be witness, and this oak. said he
That I never shall enjoy a woman but thee.

And here where he left her a weeping full sore,
Poor creature she never got sight of him more,
For in a short time thereafter he went to the sea,
And left sight of Britain with a tear in his eye.

He went to America, their orders were so,
There prov'd a gallant soldier, and valour did show,
That for his behaviour they ne'er could him blame,
From a corporal at last to a serjeant became.

PART I I I.

Being near Fort Niagara, in the year fifty-nine,
On the thirteeth of July, as he always did incline
To frequent the green-wood, or some distant place,
To breathe out his sorrows his mind to solace.

Amongst the savage Indians, alas ! here he fell,
But how he was murder'd we cannot well tell ;
For on the next morning they found him their dead,
And an Indian lay by him wanting the head.

Cut off by his broadsword as they understood,
As there all around him was nothing but blood :
Five wounds in his body, his hair scalpt away,
His clothes, sword, and pistol, of all made a prey.

And one of his fingers from his hand they had cut,
The one with the gold ring from his lover he got :
On that very moment, now in Scotland we hear,.
He a dreadful spectre to his love did appear.

And as she was weeping under the green oak,
He quickly past by her and not a word spoke ;
Yet shaking that hand where the ring he did wear,
Which wanted a finger, and blood dropping there.

Whereat the young lady was struck with amaze,
And rose to run after and on him to gaze,
As she knew it was Gregor, but how in that place,
It made her to wonder and dread the sad case.

With terror and grief home she did retire,
And spent the whole night in weeping and prayer,
So early next morning she rose with the sun,
Went back to the green oak to weep all alone.

For always she esteem'd that place, as we hear,
As on it she got the last sight of her dear,
And as she sat weeping and tearing her hair,
Again the pale spectre to her did appear.

And with a wild aspect it stared in her face,
Then said, O dear Katty, do not me embrace,
For I'm but a spirit, tho' shining in blood,
My body lies murdered in a far foreign wood.

Two wounds in my body, and three in my side,
With hatchets and arrows they're both deep & wide,
My scalp and fine hair for a premium is sold,
And also my finger with the ring of pure gold.

Which you threw upon it as a mark of true love,
Love's stronger than death for it does not remove ;
For my earnest desire is for you, my dear,
And till you are with me, I'll still wander here ;

For this world's but vanity, all's but a vain show,
It's nought to the pleasure where we are to go
She went to embrace being all of a fright,
But he in a moment vanish'd out of her sight.

Then home in great horror to her father did run,
Cried Oh ! cruel Father, now what have you done,
Gregor lov'd Gregor came to me in blood,
And his body lies murdered in an American wood

He show'd me his wounds and each bleeding sore,
And therefore my pleasures on earth are no more ;
Her father look'd at her as one being amaz'd,
Then said, my dear Katty, your brains they are craz'd

And still she maintain'd it, and cried like a child,
Never was seen for to laugh nor to smile ;
All doctors came to her, whose skill was in vain,
But still gave opinion she was sound in the brain.

Her body decayed, und her face wan and pale,
She soar'd to her true love beyond dearth's dark vale
First her, then her mother, in one night expired :
I hope she enjoys the bliss she desired.

Now the old father he cries bereft of all joys,
Tho' plenty of gold, he has neither girls nor boys,
Let all cruel parents to this then take heed,
His pretty young daughter is now with the dead.

The Jew's Daughter.

THE rain runs down thro' Mirry-land toune,
    Sae dois it doune the Pa :
Sae dois the lads of Mirry-land toune,
    Quhan they play at the ba.

Then out and cam the Jewis dochter,
    Said, Will ye cum in dine !
I winna cum in, I winna cum in,
    Without my play-feres nine.

Scho pow'd an apple reid and white
    To intice the young thing in :
Scho pow'd an apple white and reid,
    And that the sweit bairne did win.

And scho has taine out a little pen-knife,
    And low down by her gair,
Scho has twin'd the zoung thing of his life ;
    A word he neir spake mair.

And out and cam the thick thick bluid,
    And out and cam the thin;
And out and cam the bonny heart's bluid:
    Their was nae life left in.

Scho laid him on a dressing boarde,
    And drest him like a swine,
And laughing said, Gae now and play
    With zour sweet play-feres nine.

Scho row'd him in a cake of lead,
    Bade him ly still and sleip.
Scho cast him in a deip draw-well,
    Was fifty fathom deip.

Quhan bells were rung, and mass was sung,
    And every lady went hame:
Than ilk lady had her zoung sonne,
    But lady Helen had nane.

Scho row'd her mantil hir about,
    And sair sair gan she weip:
And she ran into the Jewis castel,
    Quhan they were all asleip.

My bonny Sir Hew, my pretty Sir Hew,
    I pray thee to me speik:
"O lady rinn to the deep draw-well
    Gin ze your sonne wad seik."

Lady Helen ran to the deip draw-well,
    And kneel'd upon her knee;
My bonnie Sir Hugh gin ze be here,
    I pray ze speik to me.

The lead is wondrous heavy, mither,
  The well is wondrous deip,
A keen pen-knife sticks in my hert,
  A word I downae speik.

Gae hame, gae hame, my mother deir,
  Fetch me my winding-sheet,
And at the back o' Mirry-land toune,
  Its there we twa sall meet.

Cruel Lammikin.

Lammikin was as gude a mason
  As ever hewed a stane;
He biggit Lord Weire's castle,
  But payment gat he nane.

Sen ye winna gie me my guerdon, lord,
  Sen ye winna gie me my hire,
This gude castle, sae stately built,
  I sall gar rock wi' fire.

Sen ye winna gie me my wages, lord,
  Ye sall hae cause to rue.
And syne he brewed a black revenge,
  And syne he vowed a vow.—

The Lammikin sair wroth, sair wreth,
  Returned again to Downe;
But or he gaed, he vow'd and vow'd,
  The castle should sweep the ground,—

O byde at hame, my gude lord Weire,
    I weird ye byde at hame;
Gang na to this day's hunting,
    To leave me a' alane.

Yae night, yae night, I dreamt this bower
    O red red blude was fu';
Gin ye gang to this black hunting,
    I sall hae cause to rue.

Wha looks to dreams, my winsome dame?
    Nae cause hae ye to fear;
And syne he kindly kissed her cheek,
    And syne the starting tear.—

Now to the gude green-wood he's gane,
    She to her painted bower;
But first she closed the windows and doors
    Of the castle, ha', and tower.

They steeked doors, they steeked yetts,
    Close to the cheek and chin;
They steeked them a' but a wee wicket,
    And Lammikin crap in.

Where are a' the lads o' this castle?
    Says the Lammikin;
They are a' wi' lord Weire hunting,
    The false nourice did sing.

Where are a' the lasses o' this castle?
    Says the Lammikin;
They are a' out at the washing,
    The false nourice did sing.

But where's the lady o' this house?
    Says the Lammikin;
The only bairn lord Weire aughts,
    The false nourice did sing.

Lammikin nipped the bonnie babe,
    While loud false nourice sings;
Lammikin nipped the bonnie babe,
    Till high the red blude springs.

Still my bairn, nourice,
    O still him if ye can.
He will not still, madam,
    For a' his father's lan'.

O gentle nourice still my bairn,
    O still him wi' the keys;
He will not still, fair lady,
    Let me do what I please.

O still my bairn, kind nourice,
    O still him wi' the ring.
He will not still, my lady,
    Let me do any thing.

O still my bairn, gude nourice,
    O still him wi' the knife.
He will not still, dear mistress mine,
    Gin I'd lay down my life.

Sweet nourice, loud loud cries my bairn,
    O still him wi' the bell.
He will not still, dear lady,
    Till ye cum down yoursell.

The first step she stepped,
    She stepped on a stane,
The next step she stepped,
    She met the Lammikin.

And when she saw the red red blude,
    A loud skreich skreiched she,—
O monster, monster, spare my child,
    Who never skaithed thee!

O spare, if in your bluidy breast
    Abides not heart of stane!
O spare, an ye sall hae o' gold
    That ye can carry hame!

I carena for your gold, he said,
    I carena for your fee,
I hae been wranged by your lord,
    Black vengeance ye sall drie.

Here are nae serfs to guard your ha's,
    No trusty spearmen here;
In yon green-wood they sound the horn,
    And chace the doe and deer.

Tho' merry sounds the gude green-wood
    Wi' huntsmen, hounds, and horn,
Your lord sall rue ere sets yon sun
    He has done me skaith and scorn.

O nourice, wanted ye your meat,
    Or wanted ye your fee,
Or wanted ye for any thing
    A fair lady could gie?

I wanted for nae meat, lady,
    I wanted for nae fee ;
But I wanted for a hantle
    A fair lady could gie.

Then Lammikin drew his red red sword,
    And sharped it on a stane,
And through and through this fair lady,
    The cauld cauld steel is gane.

Nor lang was't after this foul deed
    Till lord Weire comin hame,
Thocht he saw his sweet bairn's bluid
    Sprinkled on a stane.

I wish a' may be weel, he says,
    Wi' my lady at hame ;
For the rings upon my fingers
    Are bursting in twain.

But mair he looked, and dule saw he,
    On the door at the trance,
Spots o' his dear lady's bluid
    Shining like a lance.—

There's bluid in my nursery,
    There's bluid in my ha',
There's bluid in my fair lady's bower,
    An' that is warst of a'.

O sweet sweet sang the birdie
    Upon the bough sae hie,
But little cared false nourice for that,
    For it was her gallows tree.

Then out he set and saw his braw men,
   Rode a' the country roun',
Ere lang they fand the Lammikin
   Had sheltered near to Downe.

They carried him a' airts o' wind,
   And muckle pain had he,
At last before lord Weire's yett
   They hanged him on the tree.

The Faithless Captain.

ALL young maidens pray a while draw near,
   I a tragic story have to tell,
'Twill make your hearts to bleed when I do proceed,
   And for a truth has lately befal.
In London city fair, liv'd a maiden there,
   Blest with wit and charming beauty bright,
Unto a lady fair she a servant were,
   And the lady in her took delight.

She had a son we hear, who a captain was,
   A ship the Burford call'd, he did command,
And it was told to the Indies bound,
   And to forsake the British land.
His mother's waiting-maid has his heart betrayed,
   And he great kindness to her did bear,
Tho' she was but poor he did her adore,
   But at length he did her heart insnare.

Rich gold and silver bright on his heart's delight,
    With fine presents daily he would bestow,
Cloth'd her in rich array like the queen of May,
    But at last he proved her overthrow.
The joyful day we hear it appointed was
    For the marriage as you shall find,
Men have many a snare for the maidens fair,
    And it's hard for maids for to trust mankind.

The night before they married were to be,
    He unto the maiden fair did come,
Saying, my heart's delight go with me to-night,
    About some business that I must do.
To a tavern he took the maid straightway,
    She poor innocent did think no ill,
With wine, as we hear, her senses did insnare,
    Thus, the traitor had his wretched will.

But when the morning fair did then appear,
    And gentle sleep her senses did restore,
Finding thus her charms enfolded in his arms,
    Down her cheeks the crystal tears did pour.
My heart's opprest with grief finding no relief,
    Since a victim to your lust I've fell,
And my virgin bloom you have cropt so soon,
    All joy and pleasure I bid farewel.

Will you marry me sir, as you did say?
    This day you know the knot was to be tied,
For ever I'm undone, now my honour's gone,
    I'm afraid I never shall be your bride.
Then he did thus swear, fear not my only dear,
    Tho' your charming body I have enjoyed,
If I forsake my dear, heavens be severe,
    May all the substance I have be destroyed.

D

The ship that I command when I leave this land
    May it never more return again;
And my silent tomb in my youthful bloom,
    Be within the deep and the raging main.
But first I'll go to sea e'er I married be,
    To seek for honour and renown;
She said my heart did dread I should not be wed,
    Now my virgin honour is gone.

With many vows and oaths he from her arose,
    And soon on board the ship he did steer,
The beauteous damsel bright went that very night
    And bought her man's apparel for to wear.
Her charming locks of hair white as lilies were,
    She cut off that none might her know,
Drest like a sailor bright she goes that same night,
    To enter the rendezvous she did go.

She was tall and trim and straight in every limb,
    Her shape and dress together did agree,
The crew at her did gaze, the lieutenant says,
    Young man was ever you at the sea?
No, kind sir, said she, but if you'll enter me,
    I soon shall become a sailor bold,
For I've a mind to go where stormy winds do blow
    And to seek for honour and bright gold.

She was entered straight for second mate,
    And on board in a little time did go,
For the Indies they soon did sail away,
    The captain his true love did not know.
Once upon a day he to her did say,
    Mate, your person doth much appear
Just like a love of mine, I think many a time,
    When I gaze on you my dear.

She was my mother's maid, I her heart betrayed,
    And now I have left her to grieve alone,
And I wish that she soon may married be,
    To some other man e'er I return.
These were piercing darts to her tender heart,
    With a sigh from him she turned away,
Revenge ye gods, said she, on this perjur'd he,
    Whose cruelty my honour did betray.

Now comes the tragic part enough to pierce a heart,
    As soon's she found herself with child to be,
This struck her heart with fear no one being near,
    To help her in her sad extremity.
The ship's crew we hear did love her dear,
    Soon the charming loving second mate
Did appear at last big about the waist,
    And forth from her eye brought many a tear.

The captain soon took notice of the mate,
    One day sleeping in her cabin as she was,
The captain being there by her breast so fair
    Thought indeed she must a woman be.
The more on her he gaz'd the more he was amaz'd,
    He perfectly thought her face he knew,
He said reveng'd he'd be if it should be she,
    So out of the cabin straight he flew.

He call'd the surgeon straight, and said call the mate
    She trembling to the captain straight did come,
He said, I plainly see madam who you be,
    I shall be revenged for this you've done.
At his feet she fell upon her knees,
    And said do not be so severe,
It's for the love of thee that I sail'd the sea,
    Pity this distress, O dearest dear.

You have been you know, my sad overthrow,
    I did little think with child I were,
But since it is so, heaven some favour show,
    Pity a distressed creature here.
Arise and go from me, he to her did say,
    See none of this matter you let know,
Soon as ever we come in sight of land,
    I am resolved that you on shore do go.

She said my dearest dear be not so severe,
    Call to mind the oath that you made to me,
And how you did betray my virginity,
    The day before we married were to be.
Do not from me depart in this wild desart,
    Bury me in the watery main,
Freely I'd comply this moment to die,
    By the man I love let me be slain.

As this she spake tears bedewed her cheek,
    Earnestly he on her did gaze,
He unto her did say and made this reply,
    Of these arms dear Molly make your grave.
I'll not be cruel to such constancy,
    Nothing I'll refuse that I can do,
But as you are in distress heavens know the best,
    My dearest what shall become of you.

We are far from shore now the billows roar,
    The doctor now your comforter must be,
The minister I'll tell what has you befal,
    And we'll be married upon the sea.
The men all confused soon as they heard the news,
    And mov'd with pity for the tender fair,
And so we do hear they were married there,
    Ere e'er the morning light did appear.

But still as you shall find fortune prov'd unkind,
    These two lovers for to divide;
As he was sleeping by his love so fair,
    Boreas blew and dreadful storms arose.
All hands aloft they run dangers for to shun,
    While the swelling bosom of the sea
Toss them mountains high they for help do cry,
    To the Lord in their extremity.

The crew were in fear seeing danger near,
    Expecting every moment for to die,
The men all employed for to save their lives,
    As on a rock the gallant ship did lie.
This woman on the deck came amongst the rest,
    In the hurry overboard she fell;
No one could her save, the sea was her grave,
    A tragic story her love for to tell.

The powers did decree they should saved be,
    By the waves they from the rock were driven,
The storms abated were to their comfort there,
    For this kind fortune they thanked heaven.
But the captain cried where's my loving bride,
    Having look'd, but no one could her see,
For O unlucky day she was cast away,
    At this he wrung his hands most bitterly.

No rest could he take but was upon the deck,
    And earnestly of heaven he did implore,
That he her corpse might see floating on the sea,
    To gaze his last on her he did adore.
When two days were past he espied her at last,
    Her fair body floating on the main,
O Neptune kind said he thus to favour me,
    With a sight of my true love again.

Now like Leander fair I'll go to my dear,
    Evermore within her arms for to sleep,
'Twas for the sake of me she sailed the sea,
    And made her tomb in the deep.
Her love to relate I will share her fate,
    The gods unto my vows now witness be.
Many of the men thought to save him then,
    But the vital spark long'd to be free.

The swelling waves now became their graves,
    They afterwards were seen no more ;
Young men a warning take how your vows ye break
    Or it will grieve your hearts full sore.

The Gosport Tragedy.

In Gosport of late a young damsel did dwell,
For wit and for beauty did many excel,
A young man did court her for to be his dear,
And he by his trade was a ship-carpenter.

He said, my dear Molly, if you will agree,
And now will consent love, for to marry me,
Your love it will ease me of sorrow and care,
If you will but marry a ship-carpenter.

With blushes more charming than roses in June,
She answered sweet William, to wed I'm too young,
For young men are fickle I see very plain,
If a maid she is kind they'll her quickly disdain.

They'll flatter her how her charms they adore,
If they gain her consent they'll care for us no more,
The most beautiful woman that ever was born,
If a man has enjoyed her—her beauty he'll scorn.

My charming sweet Molly why do you say so?
Thy beauty's the haven to which I must go,
And if in that channel I chance for to steer,
I there will cast anchor, and stay with my dear.

I ne'er will be cloy'd with the charms of my love.
My heart is as true as the sweet turtle dove,
And all that I crave is to marry my dear,
And when you're my own no danger I'll fear.

The life of a virgin, sweet William, I prize,
For marriage brings sorrow and trouble likewise,
I'm loth for to venture and therefore forbear,
For I will not marry a ship-carpenter.

But yet all in vain he his suit did deny,
For still unto love he's forc'd her to comply,
At length with his cunning he did her betray,
Unto lewd desires he led her astray.

But when with child this young damsel did prove,
The tidings directly she sent to her love,
And by the heavens he swore to be true,
Saying I'll marry none other but you.

This past on a while, at length we do hear,
The king wanted sailors, to the sea he must steer,
Which griev'd the young damsel indeed to the heart,
To think with sweet William so soon for to part.

She said, my dear William, e'er you go to sea,
Remember the vows which you made unto me,
And if you leave me, I ne'er shall have rest,
And why will you leave me with sorrow opprest?

The kindest expressions to her he did say,
I'll marry my Molly e'er I go away,
And if that to me to-morrow you'll come,
The priest shall be brought love, and all shall be done

With kindest embraces they parted that night,
She went for to meet him next morning at light,
He said, my dear charmer, you must go with me,
Before we are married, a friend for to see.

He led her thro' groves and vallies so deep,
At length this fair creature began for to weep,
Saying, William, I fancy you lead me astray,
On purpose my innocent life to betray.

He said that is true, and none can you save,
For I all this night have been digging your grave,
Poor harmless creature when she heard him say so,
Her eyes like a fountain began for to flow.

A grave and a spade standing by she did see,
And said, must that be a bridal-bed to me?
O perjured creature, the worst of all men,
Heaven will reward you when I'm dead and gone.

O pity my infant, and spare my sweet life,
Let me go distressed if I'm not your wife;
O take not my life, lest my soul you betray,
Must I in my bloom be thus hurried away?

Her hands white as lilies, in sorrow she wrung,
Intreating for mercy, saying what have I done,
To you my dear William, what makes you severe,
To murder your true love that loves you so dear?

He said there's no time for disputing to stand,
And instantly taking the knife in his hand,
He pierced her heart while the blood it did flow,
And into the grave the fair body did throw.

He cover'd the body and home he did come,
Leaving none but the birds her death to bemoan,
On board of the Bedford he enter'd straightway,
Which lay at Portsmouth, and bound for the sea.

For carpenter's mate he was enter'd we hear,
Fit for the voyage away there to steer,
But as in the cabin one night he did lie,
The voice of his true love he heard for to cry,—

O perjured William, awake now and hear,
The words of your true love who lov'd you so dear,
The ship out of Portsmouth it never shall go,
Till I am revenged of my sad overthrow.

This spoken, she vanish'd with shrieks and cries,
The flashes of lightning did dart from her eyes,
Which put the ship's crew in a terrible fear,
Tho' none saw the ghost, the voice they did hear.

Charles Stewart, a man of courage so bold,
One night as he was going down to the hold,
A beautiful creature to him did appear,
And she in her arms had a baby so fair.

Being merry with drink, he goes to embrace
The charms of this so lovely a face;
But to his surprise she vanis'd away,
He went to the captain without more delay:

He told him the story, which when he did hear,
He said, now some of my men I do fear
Has done some murder, and if it be so,
Our ship's in great danger, if to sea she does go.

Then on a time his merry men all,
Into the great cabin to him he did call,
And said, my brave sailors, these news that I hear,
Do really surprise me with sorrow and fear.

The ghost which appears to my men in the night,
And all my brave sailors does sorely affrigt,
I fear has been wronged by some of our crew,
And therefore the person I fain would know.

Then William astonis'd did tremble and fear,
And began by the Powers above for to swear,
He nothing at all of the matter did know,
But as from the captain away he did go,

Unto his surprise his true love did see,
With that he immediately fell on his knee,
Saying, here is my true love, O where shall I run?
O save me, or else my poor soul is undone.

The murder he did confess out of hand,
Saying here before me my Molly doth stand;
Poor injured ghost thy pardon I crave,
And soon shall follow thee down to the grave.

There's none but the wretch did behold this sad sight
Then raving distracted, he died in the night:
But when that her parents those tidings did hear,
They sought for the body of their daughter so dear.

Near a place in Southampton, in a valley so deep,
The body was found, while many did weep,
At the fate of the damsel and baby so fair,
In Gosport Church-yard, they bury'd her there.

I hope this will be a warning to all
Young men, who innocent maids do enthral;
You young men be constant and true to your love,
And blessings will 'tend you, be sure, from above.

Rosanna's Overthrow.

Young virgins fair of beauty bright,
    And you that are of Cupid's fold,
Unto my tragedy give ear,
    For it's as true as e'er was told.
In Oxford liv'd a lady fair,
    The daughter of a worthy knight,
A gentleman who lived near,
    Was enamour'd with her beauty bright.

Rosanna was this maiden's name,
    The flower of all fair Oxfordshire.
This gentleman a courting came,
    Begging of her to be his dear,

Her youthful heart to love inclin'd,
    Young Cupid bent his golden bow,
And left his fatal dart behind,
    Which prov'd Rosanna's overthrow.

Within the pleasant groves they walk'd,
    And vallies where the lambs do play;
Sweet pleasnt tales of love they talk'd,
    To pass away the summer day.
My charming lovely Rose, said he,
    See how the pleasant flowers spring,
The pretty birds on every tree,
    With melody the groves do ring.

I nothing want for to delight
    My soul, but those sweet charms of thine,
My heart is fix'd, therefore my dear,
    Like the turtle-dove let us combine.
Let me embrace my heart's delight,
    Within this pleasant bower here;
This bank of violets for our bed,
    Shaded with these sweet roses fair.

She said, what can you mean, I pray,
    I am a noble lady born?
What signifies my beauty bright,
    A trifle, when my honour's gone.
My parents they will me disdain,
    Young virgins they will me deride,
Oh! do not prove my overthrow,
    If you love me, stay till your bride.

Sweet angel bright, I here do vow
    By all the powers that are divine,
I'll ne'er forsake my dearest dear,
    The girl that does my soul confine;
And if that you will me deny,
    This sword shall quickly end my woe.
Then from her arms he straightway
    In fury, out his sword he drew;

Her hands as white as lilies fair,
    Most dreadfully she then did wring,
She said, my death's approaching near,
    Would I pity take and comfort him,
It only brings my fatal fall,
    'Tis I who must receive the wound:
The crimson dye forsook her cheeks,
    At's feet she dropp'd upon the ground.

This innocence he did betray,
    Full sore against her chaste desire;
True love is a celestial charm,
    The flame of lust a raging fire.
But when her senses did revive,
    He many vows and oaths did make,
That he'd for ever true remain,
    Her company would not forsake.

PART II.

Now virgins in the second part,
    Observe this lady's fatal end.
When once your virtue is betray'd,
    You've nothing young men will commend.

After the traitor had his will,
    He never did come near her more,
And from her eyes both day and night,
    For's sake the crystal tears did pour.

Into a mourning valley she
    Would often wander all alone,
And for the jewel she had lost
    In the bower would often mourn.
Oh! that I were some pretty bird,
    That I might fly to hide my shame;
O silly maid, for to believe
    The fair delusions of a man.

The harmless lamb that sports and plays,
    The turtle constant to his mate,
Nothing so wretched is as I,
    To love a man that does me hate.
I will to him a letter send,
    Remind him of the oaths he made
Within that shady bower, where
    My tender heart he first betray'd.

Her trembling hand a letter wrote,
    My dearest dear what must I do?
Alas! what have I done, that I
    Forsaken am now by you!
I could have many a lord of fame,
    who little knows my misery;
I did forsake a worthy knight
    All for the love I bore to thee.

And now my little infant dear
    Will quickly spread abroad my shame,
One line of comfort to me send,
    E'er I am by your cruelty slain.
This answer he to her did send,
    Your insolence amazes me,
To think that I should marry one
    With whom, before, I have been free.

Indeed I'll not a father be
    Unto a bastard you shall bear,
So take no further thought of me,
    No more from you pray let me hear.
When she this letter did receive,
    She wrung her hands and wept full sore;
And every day she still would range,
    To lament within the pleasant bower.

The faithless wretch began to think
    How noble were her parents, dear,
He said, I sure shall punish'd be.
    Soon as the story they do hear.
The devil then he did begin
    To enter in his wretched mind;
Her precious life he then must have,
    Thus he to act the thing did find.

He many times did watch her out,
    Into the pleasant valley, where
One day he privately did go,
    When he knew she was not there.

And privately he dug a grave
    Underneath an oaken tree.
Then in the branches he did hide,
    To act this piece of cruelty.

Poor harmless soul she nothing knew,
    As usual she went there alone,
And on a bank of violets
    In mournful manner sat her down.
Of his unkindness did complain;
    At length the grave she did espy,
She rose indeed to view the same,
    Not thinking that he was so nigh.

You gentle gods so kind said she,
    Did you this grave for me prepare?
He then descended from the tree,
    Saying, strumpet now thy death is near.
O welcome, welcome, she replied,
    As long as by your hand I die,
This is a pleasant marriage bed,
    I'm ready, use your cruelty.

But the heavens bring to light
    Thy crime, and thus let it appear,
Winter and summer on this grave,
    The damask rose in bloom spring here:
Never to wither though 'tis cropp'd,
    But when thy hand do touch the same,
Then may the bloom that minute blast
    To bring to light my bitter shame.

More she'd have said, but with his sword,
    He pierc'd her tender body through;
Then threw her in the silent grave,
    Saying, now, there is an end of you.
He fill'd the grave up close again,
    With weeds the same did overspread:
Then unconcern'd he straight went home,
    Immediately went to his bed.

Her parents dear did grieve full sore,
    The loss of their young daughter fair,
Thinking she was stole away,
    To all their riches she was heir.
Twelve months after this was done,
    Thousands for a truth do know,
According as she did desire,
    On her grave a damask rose did grow.

Many wonder'd at the same,
    For in the winter it did spring,
If any one did crop the rose,
    In a moment it would grow again.
The thing it blaz'd the country round,
    And thousands went the same to see
This miracle from heaven shew,
    He 'mong the rest must curious be.

To go and see if this was true,
    But when unto the plant he came,
The beauteous rose he saw in bloom,
    And eagerly he crop'd the same.

The leaves did fall from off the bush,
    The rose within his hand did die;
He cried, 'tis fair Rosanna's blood,
    That spring up from her fair body.

Many people that were there,
    Took notice of what he did say;
They told him he'd a murder done,
    He the truth confess'd without delay.
They dug and found the body there,
    The first of April it was known,
Before a magistrate he went,
    And now in prison lies forlorn,

Till he his punishment receives,
    No doubt but he will have his due;
Young men by this a warning take,
    Perform your vows whate'er ye do.
For God does find out many ways,
    Such heinous sins to bring to light,
For murder's a most horrid sin,
    And hateful in his blessed sight.

Fair Rosamond.

When as king Henry rul'd the land,
  The second of that name,
Besides his queene he dearly lovde
  A faire and comely dame.

Most peerlesse was her beautye founde,
  Her favour, and her face;
A sweeter creature in this worlde
  Could never prince embrace.

Her crisped lockes like threades of golde,
  Appeared to each mans sight:
Her sparkling eyes, like orient pearles,
  Did cast a heavenlye light.

The blood within her chrystal cheekes
  Did such a colour drive,
As tho' the lily and the rose
  For mastership did strive.

Yea Rosamonde, fair Rosamonde,
  Her name was called so,
To whom our queene, dame Ellinor,
  Was known a deadlye foe.

The king therefore, for her defence,
  Against the furious queene,
At Woodstocke builded such a bower,
  The like was never seene.

Most curiouslye that bower was built
    Of stone and timber strong,
An hundred and fifty doors
    Did to this bower belong.

And they so cunninglye contrived
    With turnings round about,
That none but with a clue or threade,
    Could enter in or out.

And for his love and ladyes sake,
    That was so fair and bright,
The keeping of this bower he gave
    Unto a valiant knighte.

But fortune that doth often frowne
    Where she before did smile,
The kinges delighte and ladyes joy
    Full soon she did beguile;

For why, the kinges ungracious sonne,
    Whom he did high advance,
Against his father raised warres
    Within the realme of France.

But yet before our comelye kinge
    The English land forsooke,
Of Rosamonde, his lady faire,
    His fairwell thus he tooke:

My Rosamonde, my only Rose,
    That pleasest best mine eye:
The fairest flower in all the worlde
    To feed my fantasye:

The flower of mine affected heart,
　　Whose sweetness doth excelle :
My royal Rose, a thousand times
　　I bid thee now farewelle !

For I must leave my fairest flower,
　　My sweetest Rose, apace,
And cross the seas to famous France,
　　Proud rebelles to abase.

But yet, my Rose, be sure thou shalt
　　My coming shortlye see,
And in my heart, when whence I am,
　　Ile bear my rose with mee.

When Rosamonde, that ladye brighte,
　　Did hear the kinge say soe,
The sorrow of her grieved heart
　　Her outward lookes did show ;

And from her clear and crystal eyes
　　The teares gust out apace,
Which like the silver-pearled dewe
　　Ran down her comelye face.

Her lippes erst like the coral redde,
　　Did wax baith wan and pale,
And for the sorrow she conceived
　　Her vital spirits faile ;

And falling downe all in a swoone
　　Before king Henryes face,
Full oft he in his princelye arms
　　Her bodye did embrace :

And twentye times, with watery eyes,
    He kist her tender cheeke,
Untill he had revivde again
    Her senses mild and meeke.

Why grieves my Rose, my sweetest Rose?
    The kinge did often saye;
Because, quoth shee, to bloody warres
    My love must part awaye.

But since your grace on foreigne coastes
    Amongst your foes unkinde,
Must go to hazarde life and limbe.
    Why should I stay behinde?

Nay rather, let me like a page,
    Your sworde and target beare;
That on my breast the blowes may lighte,
    Which would offend you there.

Or lett mee, in your royal tent,
    Prepare your bed at nighte,
And with sweete baths refresh your grace,
    At your return from fighte.

So I your presence may enjoye,
    No toil I will refuse;
But wanting you, my life is death;
    Nay, death Ide rather chuse!

Content thyself, my dearest love;
    Thy rest at home shall bee
In Englandes sweet and pleasant Isle;
    For travel fits not thee.

Faire ladies brook not bloody warres;
 Soft peace their sexe delightes;
Not rugged campes, but courtlye boweres;
 Gay feastes, not cruell fightes.

My Rose shall safely here abide,
 With musicke passe the daye;
Whilst I, amonge the piercing pikes,
 My foes seeke far awaye.

My Rose shall shine in pearle and golde,
 Whilst Ime in armour dighte;
Gay galliards here my love shall dance,
 Whilst I my foes go fighte.

And you, Sir Thomas, whom I truste
 To bee my loves defence;
Be careful of my gallant Rose
 When I am parted hence.

And therewithal he fetcht a sigh,
 As though his heart would breake;
And Rosamonde, for very griefe,
 Not one plaine worde could speake.

And at their parting well they mighte
 In heart be grieved sore, ;
After that daye fair Rosamonde
 The kinge did see no more.

For when his grace had past the seas,
 And into France was gone,
With envious heart, queene Ellinor,
 To Woodstocke came anone.

And forth she calls this trustye knighte
    In an unhappy houre:
Who with his clue of twined threade,
    Came from this famous bower.

And when that they had wounded him,
    The queene this thread did gette,
And went where ladye Rosamonde
    Was like an angel sette.

But when the queene with steadfast eye
    Beheld her beauteous face,
She was amazed in her minde
    At her exceeding grace.

Cast off from thee those robes, shee said,
    That riche and costlye bee;
And drink thou up those deadlye draught,
    Which I have brought to thee.

Then presentlye upon her knees
    Sweet Rosamonde did falle;
And pardon of the queene shee craved
    For her offences all.

Take pity on my youthful yeares,
    Fair Rosamonde did crye;
And lett mee not with poison stronge
    Enforced bee to dye.

I will renounce my sinfull life,
    And in some clyster byde;
Or else be banisht, if you please,
    To range the worlde soe wide.

And for the fault which I have done,
  Tho' I was forced theretoe,
Preserve my life, and punish mee,
  As you think meet to doe.

And with these words, her lillie handes
  She wrung full often there;
And down along her lovelye face
  Did trickle many a teare.

But nothing could this furious queene
  Therewith appeased bee;
The cup of deadlye poison stronge,
  As shee knelt on her knee.

She gave this comely dame to drinke
  Who tooke it in her hand,
And from her bended knee arose,
  And on her feet did stand.

And casting up her eyes to heaven,
  Shee did for mercye call;
And drinking up the poison stronge,
  Her lite she lost withalle.

And when that deathe through every limbe
  Had showde its greatest spite,
Her chiefest foes did plain confesse
  She was a glorious wight.

Her bodye then they did entombe,
  When life was fled away,
At Godstowe, near to Oxford towne,
  As may be seene this day.

The Death of Leith-Hall.

It fell about a Martinmas,
  In the year sixty-three,
There happen'd in fair Scotland
  A grievous tragedy.

When a' the nobles did convene,,
  As they were wont to do,
And brave Leith-Hall among the rest
  To pay what he was due.

Four-and-twenty gentlemen
  Sat birling at the wine;
It was in Sir Archibald Campbell's house
  The quarrel did begin:

But how the quarrel did begin
  There's no one there did know;
But a dowie quarrel for Leith-Hall,
  It prov'd his overthrow.

Brave Leith-Hall went down the stair,
  Not knowing what to do;
Cruel Mayne followed him,
  And shot him thro' the brow.

He left him lying in his wounds,
  The blood was gushing down;
Cruel Mayne's fled the town,
  There's no more to be foun'.

A servant that had serv'd him lang
  Carried him to his bed.
And cover'd him wi' blankets warm,
  Great care of him he had.

The doctors they were called upon,
  To see what they could do;
The balls were found into his brain,
  He'd shot him thro' the brow.

His lady and his children dear
  Were brought before him there;
He spake some some words that gae them hope
  That they had lost before.

But all their hopes were frustrate;
  He saw but the third day;
Gentle death, that grievous ghost,
  There he did him slay.

The bells were rung, the Mass was sung.
  An' gave a doleful knell;
His corps was carried to Aberdeen
  An' laid down at Leith-Hall.

Now for the killing of Leith-Hall,
  And spilling of his blood,
Just vengeance fall from heavens high,
  And light on Mayne's head.

If brave Leith-Hall's been taen in drink,
  His sins, I hope's forgiven;
And I may safely say this day,
  His soul is safe in heaven.

I wish his soul may shine as bright
  As the sun does after rain;
Among the high meridians
  There's no sorrow nor pain.

The Baron of Braikley.

Inverey came down Deeside whistlin an playin,
He was at brave Braikleys yett ere it was dawin;
He rappit fou loudly, an wi a great roar,
Cried, cum down, cum down Braikley, an open the
Are ye sleepin Baronne, or are ye wakin? (door.
Thers sharp swords at your yett will gar your bluid
Open the yett Braikley an lat us within, (spin:
Till we on the green turf gar your bluid rin.
Out spak the brave Baronne ower the castell wa,
Are ye come to spulzie an plunder my ha?
But gin ye be gentlemen, licht an cum in,
Gin ye drink o my wine yell nae gar my bluid spin.
Gin ye be hird widdifus, ye may gang by,
Ye may gang to the lawlands and steal their fat ky,
Ther spulzie like revers o wyld kettrin clan,
Wha plunder unsparing baith houses and lan.
Gin ye be gentlemen, licht an cum in,
Thers meat an drink i my ha for every man.
Gin ye be hird widdifus ye may gang by,
Gang down to the lawlans an steal horse an ky.
Up spak his ladie at his bak where she laid,
Get up, get up Braikley, an be not afraid;
Thyre but hird widdifus wi belted plaids.
Cum kis me my Peggy, Ile nae langer stay,
For I will go out an meet Invercy.
But hand your tongue Peggy, and mak nae sic din,
For yon same hird widdifus will prove to be men.
She called on her Maries, they came to her han,
Cries, bring your rocks lassies we will them coman;

Get up, get up Braikley, and turn bak your ky,
For me an my women will them defy.
Come forth than my maidens an show them some ply
Well ficht them, an shortly the cowards will fly :
Gin I had a husband, wheras I hae nane,
He wadna ly in his bed an see his ky taen.
Thers four-an-twenty milk whit calves, twal o them (ky.
In the woods o Glentanner its ther they a ly,
Ther are goats in the Etnach, an sheep o the brae,
An a will be plundered by young Invercy.
Now hand your tongue Peggy, an gie me a gun,
Yell see me gae furth but Ile never return.
Call my bruther William, my unkl also,
My cusin James Gordon, well mount an well go.
Whan Braikley was ready an stood i thee closs,
He was the bravest Baronne that eer munted horse :
Whan a war assembld on the castell green,
Nae man like brave Braikley was ther to be seen.
Turn back bruther William, ye are a bridegroom,
We bonnie Jean Gordon the maid o the mill,
O sichin and sobbin shell seen get her fill.
Ime nae coward, brither, its kent Ime a man,
Ile fichht i your quarral as langs I can stan,
Ile ficht, my dear brither, wi heart an guid will,
An so will yung Harry that lives at the mill.
But turn, my dear brither, and nae langer stay.
Whatll cum o your ladie gin Braikley they slay ?
Whatll cum o your ladie an bonny yung son,
O whatll cum o them when Braikley is gone?
I never will turn, do ye think I will fly ?
No : here I will ficht, and here I will die.
Strik dogs, cries Invercy, an ficht till yere slayn,
For we are four hunder, ye are but four men.

Strik, strik, ye proud boaster, your honor is gone,
Your lans we will plunder, your castell well burn
At the head o the Etnach the battel began,
At little Auchoilzie they killd the first man.
First they killd ane, an syne they killd twa,
They killd gallant Braikley the flowr o them a.
They killd William Gordon an James o the Knox,
An brave Alexander the flowr o Glenmuick :
What sichin an moaning war heard i the glen,
For the Baronne o Braikley wha basely was slayn.
Came ye by te castell, an was ye in there,
Saw ye pretty Peggy tearing her hair?
Yes, I cam by Braikley, an I gaed in ther,
An ther saw his ladie braiding her hair.
She was rantin an dancin, an singin for joy,
An vowin that nicht she woud feest Invercy :
She eat wi him, drank wi him, welcomd him in,
Was kin to the man that had slayn her Baronne.
Up spak the son on the nourices knee,
Gin I live to be a man revenged Ile be.
Thers dool i the kitchen, and mirth i the ha,
The Baronne o Braikley is dead an awa.

The Earl of Aboyne.

THE Earl o' Aboyne to Old England's gone,
    An' a' his nobles wi' him ;
Sair was the heart his fair lady had,
    Because she wanna wi' him.

As she was a walking in her garden green,
    Amang her gentlewomen,
Sad was the letter that came to her,—
    Her lord was wed in Lunan.

Is this true, my Jean, she says,
    My lord is wed in Lunan?
O no, O no, my lady gay,
    For the lord o' Aboyne is comin'.

When she was looking o'er her castell wa',
    She spied twa boys comin' ;
What news, what news, my bonny boys?
    What news hae ye frae Lunan?

Good news, good news, my lady gay,
    The lord o' Aboyne is comin' ;
He's scarcely twa miles frae the place,
    Ye'll hear his bridles ringin'.

O my grooms all be well on call,
    An' hae your stables shinin' ;
Of corn an' hay spare nane this day,
    Sin the lord o' Aboyne is comin'.

My minstrels all be well on call,
    Now set your harps a tunin'
Wi' the finest springs, spare not the strings,
    Sin the lord o' Aboyne is comin'.

My cooks all be well on call,
 An' had your spits a-runnin'
Wi' the best o' roast, an' spare nae cost,
 Sin the lord o' Aboyne is comin'.

My maids all be well on call,
 An' hae your flours a-shinin';
Cover o'er the stair wi' herbs sweet air,
 Cover the flours wi' linen;
An' dress my bodie in the finest array,
 Sin the lord o' Aboyne is comin'.

Her gown was o' the guid green silk,
 Fastned wi' red silk trimmin';
Her apron was o' the guid black gaze,
 Her hood o' the finest linen.

Sae stately she stept down the stair,
 To look gin he was comin';
She called on Kate her cham'er maid,
 An' Jean, her gentlewoman,
To bring her a bottle of the best wine,
 To drink his health that's comin',

She's gaen to the close, taen him frae's horse,
 Says, ycur thrice welcome fra Lunan;
If I be as welcome hauf as ye say,
 Come kiss me for my comin';
For to-morrow should been my wedding day
 Gin Ide staid on langer in Lunan.

She turned about wi' a disdainful look
 To Jean, her gentlewoman;
If to-morrow should been your wedding day,
 Go kiss your whores in Lunan.

O my nobles all now turn your steeds,
　　I'm sorry for my comin' ;
For the night we'll alight at the bonny Bog o' Gight,
　　To-morrow tak horse for Lunan.

O Thomas my man gae after him,
　　An' spier gin I'll win wi' him ;
Yes, madam, I hae pleaded for thee,
　　But a mile ye winna win wi' him.

Here and there she ran in care,
　　And doctors wi' her dealin' ;
But in a crak her bonny heart brak,
　　And letters gaed to Lunan.

When he saw the letter sealed wi' black,
　　He fell on's horse a-weeping ;
If she be dead that I love best,
　　She has my heart a-keepin'.

My nobles all ye'll turn your steeds,
　　That comely face may see then ;
Frae the horse to the hat a' must be black,
　　And mourn for bonny Peggy Irvine.

When they came near to the place,
　　They heard the dead-bell knellin' ;
And aye the turnin' o' the bell
　　Said, come bury bonny Peggy Irvine.

Loch-in-var.

There lives a lass in yonder dale,
  In you bonny borrows town;
Her name it's Catherine Jeffrey,
  She is loved my many a ane.

Lord Loch-in-var has courted her
  These twelvemonths and a day;
With flattering words and fair speeches
  He has stown her heart away.

There came a knight from South sea bank,
  From north England I mean;
He alighted at her father's yetts,
  His stile is Lord Lymington.

He has courted her from father and mother,
  Her kinsfolk ane and aye;
But he never told the lady hersell
  Till he set the wedding day.

Prepare, prepare, my daughter dear,
  Prepare, to you I say,
For the night it is good Wednesday night,
  And the morn is your wedding day.

O tell to me father, she said,
  O tell me who it is wi',
For I'll never wed a man on earth
  Till I know what he be.

He's come a knight from the South sea bank,
  From north England, I mean;
For when he lighted at my yetts
  His stile is lord Lymington.

O where will I get a bonny boy
    Will win baith meat and fee,
And will run on to Loch-in-var,
    And come again to me?

O here am I, a bonny boy
    Will win baith hose and sheen,
And will run on to Loch-in-var
    And come right seen again.

Where ye find the brigs broken
    Bend your bow and swim;
For ye find the grass growing
    Slack your bow and run.

When ye come on to Loch-in-var
    Byde not to chap nor ca',
But set your bent bow to your breast,
    And lightly loup the wa'.

Bid him mind the words he last spake
    When we sendered on the lee;
Bid him saddle and ride full fast
    If he be set for me.

Where he found the brigs broken
    He bent his bow and swam;
Where he found the brigs broken
    He slackt his bow and ran.

When he came on to Loch-in-var,
    He did not chap nor ca';
He set his bent bow till his breast
    And lightly leapt the wa'.

What news, what news, my bonny boy,
    What news have ye to me?
Bad news, bad news, my lord, he said,
    Your lady awa' will be:

Your bidden mind the words ye last spake
    When we sendered on the lee;
Your bidden saddle and ride full fast
    Gin ye set for her be.

When he came to her father's yetts
    There he alighted down;
The cups of gold of good red wine
    Were going roun' and roun'.

Now came ye here for sport? they said,
    Or came ye here for play?
Or for a sight of our bonny bride,
    And then to boun your way?

I came not here for sport, he says,
    Nor came I here for play;
But if I had a sight of your bonny bride,
    Then I will boun my way.

When Lymington he called on her
    She wouldnot come at a';
But Loch-in-var he call on her,
    And she was not sweer to drew.

He has taen her by the milk white hand,
    And by her silken sleeve;
He has mounted her high him behind,
    He spiered nae mair their leave·

And aye she scoffed and scorned them,
  And aye she rode away;
And aye she gart the trumpet sound
  The voice of foul play:
To take the bride frae her bridegroom,
  Upon her wedding day.

As they came in by Foudlin dyke,
  And in by Foudlin stane,
There were mony gallant Englishman
  Lay gasping on the green.

Now a' you that are English lords,
  And are in England born,
Come never here to court your brides
  For fear ye get the scorn;

For aye they'll scoff and scorn you,
  And aye they'll ride away;
They'll gie you frogs instead of fish,
  And call it foul play.

Queen Eleanor's Confession.

The Queen's faen sick, and very very sick,
  Sick, and going to die;
And she's sent for twa Friars of France,
  To speak with her speedilie.

The king he said to the Earl Marischal,
    To the Earl Marischal said he,
The queen she wants two friars frae France
    To speak with her presentlie.

Will ye put on a friar's coat,
    And I'll put on another?
And we'll go in before the queen,
    Like friars both together.

But O forbid said the Earl Marischal
    That I this deed should dee,
For if I beguile Eleanor our queen,
    She will gar hang me hie.

The king he turned him round about,
    An angry man was he;
He's sworn by his sceptre and his sword
    Earl Marischal should not die.

The king has put on a friar's coat,
    Earl Marischal on another,
And they went in before the queen
    Like friars both together.

O if ye be twa friars of France,
    Ye're dearly welcome to me;
But if ye be twa London friars,
    I will gar hang you hie.

Twa friars of France, twa friars of France,
    Twa friars of France are we;
And we vow we never spake to a man
    Till we spake to your majesty.

The first great sin that e'er I did,
    And I'll tell you it presentlie,
Earl Marischal got my maidenhead,
    When coming o'er the sea.

That was a sin, and a very great sin,
    But pardoned may it be ;
All that with amendment, said Earl Marischal,
    But a quacking heart had he.

The next great sin that e'er I did,
    I'll tell you it presentlie ;
I carried a box seven years in my breast
    To poison King Henrie.

O that was a sin, and a very great sin,
    But pardoned may it be ;
All that with amendment, said Earl Marischal,
    But a quacking heart had he.

The next great sin that e'er I did,
    I'll tell you it presentlie ;
I poisoned the lady Rosamond,
    And a very good woman was she.

See ye not yon twa bonny boys
    As they play at the ba' ;
The eldest of them is Marischal's son,
    And I love him best of a' ;
The youngest of them is Henrie's son,
    And I love him none at a':

For he is headed like a bull, a bull,
    He is backed like a boar ;
Then by my sooth, King Henrie said,
    I love him the better therefor.

The king has cast aff his friar's coat,
    put on a coat of gold;
The queen she's turned her face about,
    She could not's face behold.

The king then said to Earl Marischal,
    To the Earl Marischal said he,
Were it not for my sceptre and sword,
    Earl Marischall, ye should die.

The Savage Blackamoor.

In Rome a nobleman did wed
    A virgin of great fame,
A fairer creature never did
    Dame nature ever frame,
By whom he had two children fair,
    Whose beauty did excel,
And were their parents' only joy,
    They lov'd them both so well.

This lord he lov'd to hunt the buck,
    The tiger and the boar,
And still for swiftness always took,
    With him a Blackamoor.
Which Blackamoor within the wood,
    His lord he did offend;
For which he did him then correct,
    In hopes he would amend.

The day it grew unto an end,
  Then homewards he did haste,
Where with his lady he did rest
  Until the night was past.
Then in the morning he did rise,
  And did his servants call,
A hunting he provides to go,
  And they were ready all;

To ease his toil the lady did
  Entreat him not to go,
Alas! good lady; then quoth he,
  Why art thou grieved so?
Content thyself, I will return
  To thee, with speed again:
Good father, quoth the little babes,
  With us here still remain.

Farewell, dear children, I will go,
  A fine thing for to buy;
But they therewith, nothing content,
  Aloud began to cry.
The mother takes them by the hand
  Saying, come go with me,
Unto the highest tower where
  Your father you shall see.

The blackamoor perceiving now
  He then did stay behind,
His lord to be a hunting gone,
  He then did call to mind—

My master he did me correct,
    My fault not being great,
Now of his wife I'll be reveng'd,
    She shall not me intreat.

The place was moted round about,
    The bridge he did up draw,
The gates he bolted very fast,
    Of none he stood in awe.
He up into the tower went,
    The lady being there,
Who, when she saw his countenance grim
    She straight began to fear.

But now my trembling heart it quakes,
    To think what I must write,
My senses all begin to fail,
    My soul it doth affright.
Yet must I make an end of this,
    Which, ere I have begun,
Will make sad the hardest heart,
    Before that I have done.

This wretch unto the lady went
    And her with speed did will,
His lust forthwith to satisfy,
    His revenge for to fulfill.
The lady she amazed was
    To hear the villain speak,
Alas! quoth she, what shall I do?
    With grief my heart will break.

With that he took her in his arms,
    She straight for help did cry,
Content yourself, lady, he said,
    Your husband is not nigh.

The bridge is drawn, the gates are shut,
  Therefore come lie with me,
Or else I do protest and vow
  Thy butcher I will be.
The crystal tears ran down her face,
  Her children cried amain,
And sought to help their mother dear,
  But all it was in vain :

For that egregious filthy rogue
  Her hands behind her bound,
And then by force with all his might,
  He threw her on the ground.
With that she shrieks, her children cried,
  And such a noice did make,
The town folks hearing her lament,
  Did seek their parts to take.

But all in vain, no way was found,
  To help this lady's need,
Who cried to them most pitiously
  O help, O help, with speed.
Some ran unto the forest wide,
  Her lord home for to call,
And they that stood still did lament
  This gallant lady's fall.

With speed her lord came posting home,
  He could not enter in,
His lady's cries did pierce his heart.
  To call he did begin,—
O hold thy hand thou savage Moor,
  To hurt her do forbear,
Or else be sure, if I do live,
  Wild horses shall thee tear.

With that the rogue ran to the wall,
    He having had his will,
And brought one child unto the wall
    His dearest blood to spill.
The child seeing his father there,
    To him for help did call,
O father help my mother dear,
    We shall be killed all.

The father fell upon his knees
    And did the Moor intreat,
To save the life of his poor child,
    Whose fear was then so great.
But this vile wretch, the little child
    By both the heels did take,
And dash'd his brains against the wall,
    While parents' hearts did ake.

That being done, away he ran
    The other child to fetch,
And pluck'd it from the mother's breast
    Most like a cruel wretch.
Within one hand a knife he brought,
    The child within the other,
And holding it against the wall,
    Saying, thus shall die thy mother.

With that he the throat did cut,
    Then to the father call,
To look how he the same did cut,
    Then down the head did fall.
This done, he threw it down the wall
    Into the mote so deep,
Which made the father wring his hands,
    And grievously to weep.

The mother then he next did take,
  Who was near dead with fear,
Yet this vile wretch most cruelly
  Did drag her by the hair.
He drew her to the very wall,
  Which, when his lord did see,
Then presently he cried out,
  And fell upon his knee;

Quoth he, if thou wilt save her life
  Whom I do love so dear,
I will forgive thee all that's past,
  Though they concern me near.
O save her life, I thee beseech,
  O save her life, I pray,
And I will grant thee what thou wilt
  Demand of me this day.

Well quoth the Moor, I do regard
  The moan that thou dost make,
If thou wilt grant what I request,
  I'll save her for thy sake.
O save her life, and then demand
  Of me what thing thou wilt:
Cut off thy nose, and not one drop
  Of her blood shall be spilt.

With that this noble lord did take
  A knife into his hand,
And there his nose did quite cut off,
  In place where he did stand.
Now I have bought my lady's life,
  Then to the Moor did call:
Then take her, quoth the wicked rogue,
  And down he let her fall!

Which, when this gallant lord did see,
    His senses did him fail;
Though many sought to save his life,
    Yet all could not prevail.
When as the Moor did see him dead,
    Then he did laugh amain,
At them who for this gallant lord
    And lady did complain.

Quoth he, I know you'll torture me,
    If that you could me get,
But all your threats I do not fear,
    Nor yet regard one whit.
Wild horses should my body tear,
    I know it to be true;
But I'll prevent you of that sport,
    Then down himself he threw.

Too good a death for such a wretch,
    A vallain void of fear:
And thus did end as sad a tale,
    As ever man did hear!

Lord Thomas and fair Eleanor.

Lord Thomas was a bold forester,
    And a chaser of the king's deer,
Fair Eleanor was a fine woman,
    And lord Thomas he loved her dear.

Come riddle my riddle, dear mother, he said,
    And riddle us both in one,
Whether I shall marry with fair Eleanor,
    And let the brown girl alone.

The brown girl she's got land, she says,
    Fair Eleanor she has got none;
Therefore I charge thee on my blessing,
    Bring me the brown girl home.

But as it befel on a holiday,
    As many more do beside,
Lord Thomas he went to fair Eleanor,
    That should have been his bride.

But when he came to fair Eleanor's bower,
    He knocked at the pin,
Then who was so ready as fair Eleanor
    To let lord Thomas in?

What news, what news, lord Thomas, she said,
    What news hast thou brought unto me?
I am come to bid thee to my wedding,
    And that is sad news for thee.

O heaven forbid, lord Thomas, she said,
    That such thing should be done;
I thought to have been the bride myself,
    And thou to have been the bridegroom.

Come riddle my riddle, dear mother, she said,
    And riddle it all in one,
Whether I shall go to lord Thomas's wedding,
    Or whether I shall let it alone?

There's many that are our friends, daughter,
    And many that are our foes;
Therefore I charge thee on my blessing,
    To lord Thomas's wedding dont go.

There's many that are our friends, mother,
    If a thousand were our foes,
Betide me life, betide me death,
    To lord Thomas's I'll go.

She clothed herself in gallant attire,
    And her merry men all in green,
And as she rode through every place,
    They took her to be some Queen.

When she came to lord Thomas's gate,
    She knocked at the pin:
And who was so ready as lord Thomas,
    To let fair Eleanor in.

He took her by the lily white hand,
    And led her through the hall;
He set her in the noblest chair
    Among the ladies all.

Is this your bride, fair Eleanor said,
    Methinks she looks wond'rous brown?
Thou might'st have had as fair a woman
    As ever trod the ground.

Despise her not, lord Thomas he said,
    Despise her not unto me,
For better I love thy little finger
    Then all her whole body.

This brown girl had a little pen knife,
    Which was both keen and sharp,
And betwixt the short ribs and the long
    She prick'd fair Eleanor to the heart.

O Christ now save me, lord Thomas he said,
    Methinks thou look'st wond'rous wan,
Thou usest to look as good a colour
    As ever the sun shin'd on.

O art thou blind, lord Thomas, she said,
    Or canst thou not very well see;
Dost thou not see my own heart's blood
    Run trickling down my knee.

O dig my grave, lord Thomas replied,
    Dig it both wide and deep,
And lay fair Eleanor by my side,
    And the brown girl at my feet.

Lord Thomas he had a sword by his side,
    As he walk'd about the hall;
He cut the bride's head from her shoulders,
    And flung it against the wall.

He set his sword upon the ground
    And the point against his heart;
There never were three lovers sure
    That sooner did depart.

Lady Anne.

Fair Lady Anne sat in her bower,
    Down by the greenwood side,
And the flowers did spring, and the birds did sing,
    'Twas the pleasant Mayday tide.

But fair Lady Anne on Sir William call'd,
    With the tear grit in her e'e;
O though thou be fause, may heaven thee guard
    In the wars ayont the sea!

Out of the wood came three bonny boys,
    Upon the simmer's morn,
And they did sing, and play at the ba',
    As naked as they were born.

O seven lang years wad I sit here,
    Amang the frost and snaw,
A' to hae ane o' thae bonnie boys,
    A playing at the ba'.

Then up and spake the eldest boy,
    Now listen thou fair ladie!
And ponder well the tale I tell,
    Then make ye a choice of the three.

'Tis I am Peter, and this is Paul,
    And that ane sae fair to see,
But a twelvemonths sinsyne to Paradise came
    To join with our companie.

O I will hae the snaw-white boy,
    The bonniest of the three;
And if I were thine, by free propine,
    O what wad ye do to me?

It's I wad clead thee in silk and gowd,
  And nourice thee on my knee.
O mither! O mither! whan I was thine,
  Sic kindness I couldna see:

At love's gay call, in the baron's hall,
  Ye quaff'd the laughing wine,
While foodless days, and sleepless nights,
  In a menial's hut were mine.

Beneath the turf where now I stand,
  The fause nurse buried me;
Thy cruel pen-knife still sticks in my heart,
  And I come not back to thee!

The Bonny Earl of Murray.

Ye Highlands and ye Lawlands,
  Oh quhair hae ye been?
They hae slaine the Earl of Murray,
  And hae lain him on the green.

Now wae be to thee, Huntly!
  And quhairfore did you sae,
I bade you bring him wi' you,
  But forbade you him to slay?

He was a braw gallant,
  And he rid at the ring,
And the bonny Earl of Murray,
  Oh! he might hae been a king.

He was a braw gallant,
    And he play'd at the ba';
And the bonny of Murray
    Was the flower among them a'.

He was a braw gallant,
    And he play'd at the gluve;
And the bonny Earl of Murray,
    Oh! he was the Queenes luve.

Oh! lang will his lady
    Luke owre the castle Downe,
Ere she see the Earl of Murray
    Cum sounding throw the towne.

Clerk Colvill and the Mermaid.

CLERK COLVILL and his lusty dame
    Were walking in the garden green;
The belt around her stately waist
    Cost Clerk Colvill of pounds fifteen.

O promise me now, Clerk Colvill,
    Or it will cost ye muckle strife;
Ride never by the wells of Slanes,
    If ye wad live and brook your life.

Now speak nae mair, my lusty dame,
    Now speak nae mair of that to me;
Did I ne'er see a fair woman,
    But I wad sin with her fair body?

He's taen leave of his gay lady,
  Nought minding what his lady said;
And he's rode by the wells of Slanes,
  Where washing was a bonny maid.

Wash on, wash on, my bonny maid,
  That wash sae clean your sark of silk;
And well fa you, fair gentleman,
  Your body's whiter than the milk.

Then loud, loud cried the Clerk Colvill,
  O my head it pains me sair;
Then take, then take, the maiden said,
  And frae my sark you'll cut a gare.

Then she's gien him a little bane-knife,
  And frae his sark he cut a share;
She's ty'd it round his whey-white face,
  But aye his head it aked mair.

Then louder cried the Clerk Colvill,
  O sairer, sairer akes my head;
And sairer, sairer ever will,
  The maiden cries, till you be dead.

Out then he drew his shining blade,
  Thinking to stick her where she stood:
But she has vanish'd to a fish,
  And swam far off a fair mermaid.

O mother, mother, braid my hair;
  My lusty lady make my bed;
O brother, take my sword and spear,
  For I have seen the false Mermaid.

Sir Patrick Spens.

The King sits in Dumfermline toun,
    Drinking the blude-red wine;
O whare will I get a skeely skipper,
    To sail this ship of mine?

O up and spak an eldren knight,
    Sat at the King's right knee,
Sir Patrick Spens is the best sailor
    That ever sail'd the sea.

Our king has written a braid letter,
    And sign'd it wi' his hand,
And sent it to Sir Patrick Spens,
    Was walking on the strand.

To Noroway, to Noroway,
    To Noroway o'er the faem;
The king's daughter o' Noroway,
    It's thou maun bring her hame.

The first word that Sir Patrick read,
    Sae loud loud laughed he;
The neist word that Sir Patrick read,
    The tear blinded his e'e.

O wha is this has done this deed,
    And tauld the king o' me,
To send us out at this time o' the year
    To sail upon the sea.

Be it wind, be it weet, be it hail, be it sleet,
    Our ship maun sail the faem;
The king's daughter o' Noroway,
    It's we maun fetch her hame.

They hoysed their sails on Monendy morn,
    Wi' a' the speed they may ;
They hae landed in Noroway
    Upon a Wodensday.

They hadna been a week, a week
    In Noroway but twae,
When that the lords o' Noroway
    Began aloud to say,

Ye Scottishmen spend a' our king's goud,
    And a' our queenis fee !
Ye lie, ye lie, ye liars loud !
    Fu loud I hear you lie.

For I brought as much white monie,
    As gane my men and me ;
And I brought a half-fou o' gude red goud
    Out o'er the sea wi' me.—

Make ready, make ready, my merrymen a',
    Our good ship sails the morn.
O say no sae, my master dear,
    For I fear a deadly storm.

Late late yestreen I saw the new moon,
    Wi' the auld moon in her arm ;
And I fear, I fear, my master dear,
    That we will come to harm.

They hadna sailed a league, a league,
    A league but barely three,
When the lift grew dark, and the wind blew loud
    And gurly grew the sea.

The aukers brak, and the top-masts lap,
    It was sic a deadly storm,
And the waves came o'er the broken ship,
    Till a' her sides were torn.

O whare will I get a sailor gude,
    To take my helm in hand,
Till I get up to the tall top-mast,
    To see if I can spy land?

O here am I, a sailor gude,
    Will tak the helm in hand,
Till you go to the tall top-mast;
    But I fear you'll never spy land.

He hadna gane a step, a step,
    A step but barely ane,
When a bout flew out of our goodly ship,
    And the salt sea it came in.

Gae fetch a web o' the silken claith,
    Another o' the twine,
And wap them into our gude ship's side,
    And let na the sea cum in.

They fetched a web o' the silken claith,
    Another o' the twine,
And they wapped them roun' that gude ships side
    But still the sea cam in.

O laith, laith were our gude Scots lords,
    To weet their cork-heeled shoon;
But lang or a' the play was played,
    They wat their hats aboon.

And mony was the feather-bed,
   That flattered on the faem;
And mony was the good lord's son,
   That never mair came hame.

The ladyes wrang their fingers white,
   The maidens tore their hair,
A' for the sake o' their true loves;
   For them they'll see nae mair.

O lang, long may the ladyes sit,
   Wi' their fans into their hand,
Before they see Sir Patrick Spens
   Come sailing to the strand!

And lang, lang may the maidens sit,
   Wi' their goud kaims in their hair,
A' waiting for their ain dear loves!
   For them they'll see nae mair.

Half owre, half owre to Aberdour,
   It's fifty fathom deep.
And there lies gude Sir Patrick Spens,
   Wi' the Scots lords at his feet.

Andrew Lammie.

At Mill of Tifty lived a man,
    In the neighbourhood of Fyvie,
He had a lovely daughter fair,
    Was called bonny Annie.

Her bloom was like the springing flower
    That hails the rosy morning,
With innocence and graceful mein,
    Her beauteous form adorning.

Lord Fyvie had a trumpeter
    Whose name was Andrew Lammie,
He had the art to gain the heart
    Of Mill of Tifty's Annie.

Proper he was both young and gay,
    His like was not in Fyvie,
Nor was ane there that could compare
    With this same Andrew Lammie.

Lord Fyvie he rode by the door,
    Where lived Tifty's Annie,
His trumpeter rode him before,
    Even this same Andrew Lammie.

Her mother called her to the door,
    Come here to me my Annie,
Did e'er you see a prettier man
    Than the trumpeter of Fyvie?

Nothing she said, but sighing sore,
    Alas! for bonny Annie:
She durst not own her heart was won
    By the trumpeter of Fyvie.

At night when all went to their bed,
    All slept full soon but Annie,
Love so opprest her tender breast
    Thinking on Andrew Lammie.

Love comes in at my bed side,
    And love lies down beyond me,
Love so oppress'd my tender breast,
    And love will waste my body.

The first time me and my love met
    Was in the woods of Fyvie,
His lovely form, and speech so soft,
    Soon gain'd the heart of Annie.

He called me mistress, I said no,
    I'm Tifty's bonny Annie.
With apples sweet he did me treat,
    And kisses soft and mony,.

It's up and down in Tifty's den
    Where the burn runs clear and bonny,
I've often gane to meet my love,
    My bonny Andrew Lammie.

But now, alas! her father heard,
    That the trumpeter of Fyvie
Had had the art to gain the heart
    Of Mill of Tifty's Annie.

Her father soon a letter wrote,
    And sent it on to Fyvie,
To tell his daughter was bewitch'd
    By his servant, Andrew Lammie.

Then up the stair his trumpeter
    He called soon and shortly,
Pray tell me soon what's this you've done,
    To Tifty's bonny Annie?

Woe be to Mill of Tifty's pride,
    For it has ruined many,
They'll not have't said that she should wed
    The trumpeter of Fyvie.

In wicked art I had no part,
    Nor therein am I canny,
True love alone the heart has won
    Of Tifty's bonny Annie.

Where will I find a boy so kind,
    That will carry a letter canny,
Who will run to Tifty's town,
    Give it to my love Annie.

Tifty he has daughters three,
    Who all are wonderous bonny,
But ye'll ken her o'er a the rest,
    Give that to bonny Annie.

It's up and down in Tifty's den
    Where the burn runs clear and bonny,
There wilt thou come and I'll attend,
    My love I long to see thee.

Thou mayst come to the brig of Slugh,
    And there I'll come and meet thee.
It's there we will renew our love,
    Before I go and leave you.

My love I go to Edinburgh town,
    And for a while must leave thee;
She sighed sore, and said no more,
    But I wish that I were with you.

I'll buy to thee a bridal gown,
    My love I'll buy it bonny,
But I'll be dead ere ye come back,
    To see your bonny Annie.

If ye'll be true and constant too,
    As I am Andrew Lammie,
I shall thee wed when I come back
    To see the lands of Fyvie.

I will be true and constant too
    To thee, my Andrew Lammie,
But my bridal bed or then'll be made
    In the green church-yard of Fyvie.

The time is gone and now comes on
    My dear, that I must leave thee,
If longer here I should appear,
    Mill of Tifty he would see me.

I now for ever bid adieu
    To thee, my Andrew Lammie,
Or ye come back I will be laid
    In the green church-yard of Fyvie.

He hied him to the head of the house,
    To the house top of Fyvie,
He blew his trumpet loud and shrill,
    It was heard at Mill of Tifty.

Her father lock'd the door at night,
    Laid by the keys fu' canny,
And when he heard the trumpet sound,
    Said, your cow is lowing, Annie.

My father dear, I pray forbear,
    And reproach not your Annie.
I'd rather hear that cow to low,
    Than all the kye in Fyvie.

I would not for my braw new gown
    And all your gifts so many,
That it was told in Fyvie land
    How cruel ye are to Annie.

But if ye strike me I will cry,
    And gentlemen will hear me,
Lord Fyvie will be riding by,
    And he'll come in and see me.

At the same time the lord came in,
    He said, what ails thee, Annie?
It's all for love now I must die,
    For bonny Andrew Lammie.

Pray Mill of Tifty give consent,
    And let your daughter marry,
It will be with some higher match
    Than the trumpeter of Fyvie.

If she were come of as high a kind
    As she's advanced in beauty,
I would take her unto myself.
    And make her my own lady.

Fyvie lands are far and wide,
    And they are wonderous bonny,
But I would not leave my own true love
    For all the lands in Fyvie.

Her father struck her wonderous sore,
    As also did her mother;
Her sisters also did her scorn,
    But woe be to her brother.

Her brother struck her wonderous sore,
    With cruel strokes and many,
He broke her back in the hall door,
    For liking Andrew Lammie.

Alas! my father and mother dear,
    Why so cruel to your Annie?
My heart was broken first by love,
    My brother has broke my body.

O mother dear make me my bed,
    And lay my face to Fyvie,
Thus will I lie, and thus will die,
    For my dear Andrew Lammie.

Ye neighbours hear baith far and near,
    And pity Tifty's Annie,
Who dies for love of one poor lad,
    For bonny Andrew Lammie.

No kind of vice e'er stain'd my life,
    Or hurt my virgin honour,
My youthful heart was won by love,
    But death will me exoner.

Her mother then she made her bed,
    And laid her face to Fyvie,
Her tender heart it soon did break,
    And never saw Andrew Lammie.

Lord Fyvie he did wring his hands,
    Said, alas! for Tifty's Annie;
The fairest flower cut down by love,
    That ever sprang in Fyvie.

Woe be to Mill of Tifty's pride,
    He might have let them marry,
I should have given them both to live
    Into the lands of Fyvie.

Her father sorely now laments
    The loss of his dear Annie,
And wishes he had given consent
    To wed with Andrew Lammie.

When Andrew home from Edinburgh came,
    With muckle grief and sorrow,
My love is dead for me to-day,
    I'll die for her to-morrow.

Now I will run to Tifty's den,
    For the burn runs clear and bonny,
With tears I'll view the brig of Slugh,
    Where I parted from my Annie.

Then will I speed to the green kirk-yard,
To the green kirk-yard of Fyvie,
With tears I'll water my love's grave,
Till I follow Tifty's Annie.

The Northern Lord and Cruel Jew.

A NOBLE lord of high renown,
Two daughters had, the eldest brown,
The youngest beautiful and fair,
By chance a noble knight came there.

Her father said kind sir I have
Two daughters, which do you crave?
One that is beautiful he cried,
The noble night he then replied:

She's young, she's beautiful and gay,
And is not to be given away,
But as jewels are bought and sold,
She shall bring me her weight in gold.

The price I think ye need not grudge,
Since I will freely give as much
With her one sister, if I can
Find out some other nobleman.

With that bespoke the noble knight,
I'd sooner have the beauty bright,
At that vast rate renowned lord,
Then the other with a vast reward.

So then the bargain it was made,
But e'er the money could be paid,
He had it of a wealthy Jew,
The sum so large, the writings drew,

That if he fail'd, or miss'd the day,
So many ounces he should pay
Of his own flesh, instead of gold;
All was agreed, the sum was told

So he returned immediately
Unto the lord, where he did buy
His daughter fine, I do declare,
And paid him down the money there.

He bought her there it is well known,
Unto mankind she was his own,
By her a son he did enjoy,
A sweet and comely handsome boy.

At length the time of pay drew near,
When the knight did begin to fear,
He dreaded much the cruel Jew,
Because the money it was due.

His lady ask'd him why he griev'd?
He said my jewel I received
Such sum of money of a Jew,
And now the money it is due.

And now the day of payment's come,
I'm sure I cannot pay the sum,
He'll have my flesh weight for weight,
Which makes my grief and sorrow great.

Hush, never fear him, she replied,
We'll cross the raging ocean wide,
And so secure you from the fate :
To her request he yielded straight.

Then having pass'd the raging seas,
They travelled on, till by degrees
Unto the German court they came,
The knight, his son, and comely dame.

Unto the Emperor he told
His story of the sum of gold,
That he had borrowed of a Jew,
And that for fear of death he flew.

The Emperor he did erect
A court for them, and show'd respect
Unto his guests, because they came
From Britain, that blest land of fame.

As here he lived in delight
A Dutch lord told our English knight,
That he a ton of gold would lay
He could enjoy his lady gay.

From her the lord he was to bring
A rich and costly diamond ring,
That was to prove and testify
How he did with his lady lie.

He tries but never could obtain,
Her favour but with high disdain,
She did abhor his base intent,
So to her chamber maid he went.

And told her if she would but steal,
Her lady's ring, and to conceal
The same, and bring it to him straight,
She should enjoy a fine estate.

In hopes of such a fine reward,
The ring she stole, then the Dutch lord
Did take it to the noble knight,
Who almost swooned at the sight.

Home he goes to the lady straight.
Meeting her at the palace gate,
He flung her headlong into the mote,
And left her there to sink or float.

Soon after that in clothes of green,
She like a warlike knight was seen,
And in most gallant gay deport,
She rode unto the Emperor's court.

Now when the Emperor beheld,
Her brave deportment he was fill'd
With admiration at the sight,
Who call'd herself an English knight.

The Emperor then did reply,
We have an English knight to die
For drowning of his lady gay,
Quoth she, I'd see him if I may.

'Twas granted, so to him she came,
And calling of him by his name,
She said, kind sir, be of good cheer,
Your friend I'll be, you need not fear.

She to the Emperor did ride,
And said, now let this cause be tried
Once more, for I've a mind to save
This noble gallant from the grave.

It being done, the court was set,
The Dutch lord came seeming to fret,
About the ring seeming to fear,
How truth would make his shame appear.

And so it did, and soon they call
The maid, who on her knees did fall
Before the court, and did confess
The Dutch lord's unworthiness.

The court replied is it so?
The lady too for ought we know,
May be alive, therefore we'll stay
The sentence till another day.

Now the Dutch lord gave him a ton
Of gold, which he had justly won,
And so he did with shame and grief,
And thus the knight obtain'd relief.

The Dutch lord to revenge the spite
Upon our noble English knight,
Did send a letter out of hand,
And so the Jew did understand,

How he was in a German court,
So here upon this good report,
The Jew has cross'd the ocean wide,
Resolving to be satisfied.

Soon as e'er he fix'd his eyes,
Unto the knight in wrath he cries,
Your hand and seal I pray behold,
Your flesh I'll have instead of gold.

Said the noble knight in green,
May not your articles be seen,
Yes that they may, replied the Jew,
And I'm resolved to have my due.

So then the knight began to read,
At length she said, I find indeed
Nothing but flesh you are to have,
Answers the Jew, that's all I crave.

The poor distress'd knight was brought,
The bloody minded Jew he thought
That day to be reveng'd on him,
And part his flesh from every limb.

The knight in green said, Mr. Jew,
There's nothing else but flesh your due,
Then see no drop of blood you shed,
For if you do, off goes your head.

Pray take your due with all my heart,
But with his blood I will not part.
With that the Jew sneak'd away,
And had not one word more to say.

No sooner were these troubles past
But his wife's father came at last,
Resolving for to have is life,
For drowning his beloved wife.

Over the seas her father brought
Many brave horses, one was bought
By the pretended knight in green,
Which was the best that e'er was seen.

So to the German court he came,
Declaring such a one by name
Had drowned his fair daughter dear,
And ought to die a death severe.

They brought him from the prison then,
Guarded by many armed men,
Unto the place where he must die,
And the young knight was standing by,

Then from her side her sword she drew,
And run her gelding thro' and thro';
Her father said, why do you so?
I may, it is my own, you know.

You sold your gelding 'tis well known,
I bought it, making it my own,
And may do what I please with it;
And then to her he did submit.

Here is a man arraign'd and cast,
And brought so suffer death at last,
Because your daughter dear he slew,
Which if he did what's that to you.

You had your money when you sold
Your daughter for her weight in gold ;
Wherefore he might, it is well known,
Do what he pleased with his own.

So having chang'd her garments green,
And dress'd herself like a fair queen,
Her father and her husband straight
Both knew her, and their joys were great.

Soon they did carry the report
Unto the famous German court.
How the renowned English knight
Had found his charming lady bright.

So the Emperor and the lords of fame,
With cheerful hearts they did proclaim,
An universal joy to see,
His lady's life at liberty.

Mary's Dream.

(OLD WAY.)

The lovely moon had climbed the hill
    Where eagles big aboon the Dee,
And like the looks of a lovely dame,
    Brought joy to every bodies ee ;
A' but sweet Mary, deep in sleep,
    Her thoughts on Sandy far at sea ;
A voice drapt saftly on her ear,
    ' Sweet Mary, weep nae mair for me !'

She lifted up her waukening een,
  To see from whence the voice might be,
And there she saw her Sandy stand,
  Pale, bending on her his hollow ee!
'O Mary, dear, lament nae mair,
  I'm in death's thraws below the sea;
Thy weeping makes me sad in bliss,
  Sae, Mary, weep nae mair for me!'

'The wind slept when we left the bay,
  But soon it waked and raised the main,
And God he bore us down the deep,
  Who strave wi' him but strave in vain!
He stretched his arm and took me up,
  Tho' laith I was to gang but thee,
I look frae heaven aboon the storm,
  Sae, Mary, weep nae mair for me!'

'Take aff thae bride sheets frae thy bed,
  Which thou hast faulded down for me;
Unrobe thee of thy earthly stole—
  I'll meet wi' thee in heaven hie.
Three times the grey cock flapt his wing,
  To mark the morning lift her ee,
And thrice the passing spirit said,
  Sweet Mary, weep nae mair for me!'

Willie Wallace.

Wallace in the high highlans,
  Neither meat nor drink got he,
Said fa' me life, or fa' me death,
  Now to some town I maun be.

He's put on his short claiding,
  And on his short claiding put he,
Says fa' me life, or fa' me death,
  Now to Perth-town I maun be.

He steped o'er the river Tay,
  I wat he steped on dry land;
He wasna aware of a well-fared maid
  Was washing there her lilie hands.

What news, what news, ye well-fared maid?
  What news hae ye this day to me?
No news, no news, ye gentle knight,
  No news hae I this day to thee,
But fifteen lords in the hostage house
  Waiting Wallace for to see.

If I had but in my pocket
  The worth of one single pennie,
I would go to the hostage house,
  And there the gentlemen to see.

She put her hand in her pocket,
  And she has pull'd out half-a-crown,
Says, take ye that ye belted knight,
  'Twill pay your way till ye come down.

As he went from the well-fared maid,
    A beggar bold I wat met he,
Was cover'd wi' a clouted cloak,
    And in his hand a trusty tree.

What news, what news, ye silly auld man ?
    What news hae ye this day to gie ?
No news, no news, ye belted knight,
    No news hae I this day to thee,
But fifteen lords in the hostage house
    Waiting Wallace for to see.

Ye'll lend me your clouted cloak
    That covers you frae head to shie,
And I'll go to the hostage house,
    Asking there for some supplie.

Now he's gone to the West-muir wood,
    And there he's pull'd a trusty tree,
And then he's on to the hostage gone,
    Asking there for charitie.

Down the stair the Captain comes,
    Aye the poor man for to see ;
If ye be a captain as good as ye look
    Ye'll give a poor man some supplie ;
If ye be a captain as good as ye look,
    A guinea, this day, ye'll gie to me.

Where were ye born ye crooked carle ?
    Where were ye born, in what countrie ?
In fair Scotland I was born,
    Crooked carle that I be.

I would give you fifty pounds,
    Of gold and white monie;
I would give you fifty pounds,
    If the traitor Wallace ye'd let me see.

Tell down your money, said Willie Wallace,
    Tell down your money, if it be good,
I'm sure I have it in my power,
    And never had a better bode.

Tell down your money, said Willie Wallace,
    And let me see if it be fine,
I'm sure I have it in my power
    To bring the traitor Wallace, in.

The money was told on the table,
    Silver bright of pounds fiftie:
Now here I stand, said Willie Wallace,
    And what hae ye to say to me?

He slew the captain where he stood,
    The rest they did quack an roar;
He slew the rest around the room,
    And ask'd if there were any more.

Come cover the table, said Willie Wallace,
    Come cover the table now, make haste,
For it will soon be three lang days
    Sin I a bit o' meat did taste.

The table was not well covered,
    Nor yet was he set down to dine
Till fifteen more of the English lords
    Surrounded the house where he was in.

The guidwife she ran but the floor,
    And aye the guidman he ran ben;
From eight o'clock to four at noon,
    He has kill'd full thirty men.

He put the house in sick a swither,
    That five of them he sticket dead;
Five of them he drown'd in the river,
    And five hung in the West-muir wood.

Now he is on, to the North-Insch gone,
    Where the maid was washing tenderlie;
Now by my sooth, said Willie Wallace,
    It's been a sair day's wark to me.

He's put his hand in his pocket,
    And he has pull'd out twenty pounds,
Says, take ye that, ye well-fared maid,
    For the gude luck of your half-crown.

James Francis Edward Keith.

YE heroes all of Marischal kind,
    Who bear a timerous heart,
Hark how the woeful tidings come,
    That pierces like a dart!

Brave Keith was Earl of Marischal's son,
    Of noble blood came he;
But when the rebel crew was beat,
    He went beyond the sea.

Then into Spain he went with speed,
    Their highly was advanc'd;
But 'cause he would not Popish be,
    They daily on him scanc'd:

And all was for his principle,
    No other crime at all;
They cruelly tortur'd him to death;
    The Scot without a gall.

The Spanish king his favourite was,
    In tears thus him addrest,—
Next day the inquisition court
    Would sadly him arrest.

Brave Keith then stole away by night,
    Before the summons came;
The Spanish king conducted him
    With letters from his hand.

Then unto Berlin took his way,
    Where Protestants did reign;
And join'd in heart and hand with them,
    As there his love did hing.

But being in a bloody field,
    And wounded deep and sore;
His sword was sheath'd in Russian land,
    Resolv'd to fight no more.

Then brought to France, and homeward bound
    His wounds thought mortal still,
By mineral wells and Providence,
    He's now restored well.

But there to serve a popish prince
    His heart it stood in awe ;
To fight against his native land
    His sword vow'd ne'er to draw.

He then the Prussian court entered,
    And there field marshal made ;
And still his fame it did increase
    While he the Prussians led :

But cowardly Austrians in the night,
    Like evening wolves they came ;
(As thieves and owls act in the dark,)
    But when 'twas light they ran.

Upon Keith's quarters they began
    To murder, all asleep ;
His pickets beat, and sentrys slew,
    Who did the watches keep.

Then from his sleep, with haste he rose,
    His troops to rally, then,
But here, alas ! that hero fell
    Among the slain men.

When Prussia knew that Keith was slain,
    He cried, my father dear ;
My dearest friend, when hard bestead,
    Thy counsel still was clear.

Thou wast my cabinet of wit ;
    Thou wast my ruling plan ;
Thou wast the darling of my heart,
    O thou, dear mortal man !

Prince Frederick, of the same blood,
  Lies by thee, slain indeed;
But thou, brave Keith worth thousands ten,
  For help in time of need.

Thou wast my cabinet of wit;
  Thou wast my ruling plan;
Thou wast the darling of my heart,
  O thou, dear mortal man!

And for the sake of you, brave Keith,
  My tears I cannot dry;
My sword in peace shall ne'er be sheath'd
  Till Dann or I shall die.

Lorenzo.

Lorenzo, rich and high in power,
  Fair Rosa to the altar led;
And now it reach'd the midnight hour,
  And Rosa prest her bridal bed.

She heard the opening of the door,
  She saw around the taper's glare;
A footstep sounded on the floor,
  She cry'd, My bridegroom, art thou there?

A shrouded arm the curtain drew,
  While Rosa's heart was chill'd with fear;
Henry's pale spectre met her view,
  And cry'd, Behold the bridegroom's here!

To me your vows you gave,
  For you, false Rosa, have I died—
To my dear mansion, the cold grave,
  I come to bear away my bride!

The Death of Ella.

On Ella's cheek the rose was seen,
The tint was pure, the hue serene;
A while it bloom'd in beauty rare,
But transient was its dwelling there.
Bright was her eye of heavenly blue,
Her lips like rubies dipp'd in dew;
And sweetest melody there hung,
On the soft accents of her tongue.

But soon the storm began to low'r,
He struck the tree that held the flower:
Her lover, she drooped her head,
In sorrow o'er his lowly bed:
And fading like her cheek's soft bloom,
Sunk like a lily to the tomb:
Still will the tears soft pity gave,
Refresh the flow'rs that deck her grave.

Lord John.

Lord John he's on to England gone,
    To England gone is he;
Love John he's on to England gone,
    The king's banneret to be.

He hadna been in fair England
    O but a little while,
Till faen in love wi' the king's daughter,
    And to him she's with chile.

Now word is to the kitchen gane,
    And word is to the ha';
And word is to the king's high court,
    And that was warst of a'.

Out then spake the king himsell,
    An angry man was he;
I'll put her into prison strong,
    And starve her till she die.

Love John he's on to Scotland gone,
    I wat he's on wi' speed;
Love John he's on to Scotland gone,
    And as good was his need.

He hadna been in fair Scotland
    But a very short tide,
Till he minded on the damsel
    That lay last by his side.

Whare will I get a bonny boy
    Will win baith meat and fee,
That will run on to fair England,
    And haste him back to me?

O here am I, a bonny boy,
    Will win baith meat and fee;
That will rin on to fair England,
    And haste him back to thee.

Where ye find the grass grow green
    Ye'll slack your shoes and rin;
And when ye find the brigs broken,
    Ye'll bend your bow and swim.

And when ye come to the king's high court,
    Ye'll rin it round about,
And there ye'll see a lady gay
    At a window, looking out.

Bid her take this shirt of silk,
    Her ain hand sewed the sleeve;
Bid her come to good green-wood,
    At her parents spier nae leave.

Bid her take this shirt of silk,
    Her ain hand sewed the gair;
Bid her come to good green-wood,
    Love John he waits her there.

Where he found the grass grow green
    He slack'd his shoes and ran;
Where he fan the brigs broken,
    He bent his bow and swam.

When he came to the king's high court,
    He ran it round about;
And there he saw the lady gay
    At the window, looking out.

Ye're bidden take this shirt of silk,
    Ye're ain hand sewed the sleeve;
Ye're bidden come to good green-wood,
    At your parents spier nae leave.

Ye're bidden take this shirt of silk,
    Ye're ain hand sewed the gair;
Ye're bidden come to good green-wood,
    Love John he waits you there.

My feet are in the fetters strong,
    Instead of silken sheen;
My breast plate's of the cold iron,
    Instead of gold so fine.

But I will write a broad letter,
    And seal it with my hand,
And send it off to my love Johnny,
    And let him understand.

The first line that he looked on,
    A loud laughter laught he;
But ere he read it to the end,
    The tear blinded his ee.

O I will on to fair England
    Whatever me betide,
For to relieve the damsel
    That lay last by my side.

Out it spake his father dear,
    A noble lord was he;
If ye gang to England Johnny,
    Ye'll ne'er come back to me.

Out it spake a noble lord,
    A noble lord, I wat, was he;
Fifteen of our Scottish lords
    Will bear his honour companie.

The first town that they e'er came till
    They gart the bells be rung;
The next town that they came till,
    They gert the Mass be sung;

And when they came to the king's court
    They gart the trumpet soun;
Till the king and all his merry young men
    Did marvel at the tune.

Is this the duke of Marlborough?
    Or James, the Scottish king?
Or is it else some Scottish lord,
    Come here a visiting.

It's not the duke of Marlborough,
    Nor James, the Scottish king;
It is love John of fair Scotland,
    Come here a visiting.

If this be John of fair Scotland,
    He's dearly welcome to me;
The morn ere he eat or drink,
    High hanged he shall be.

He's taen his broadsword in his hand,
    And strip'd it o'er a stane,
Then thro' and thro' the king's high court
    With broadsword now is gane.

They fought it up, they fought it down,
   Till they were weary men;
When the blood like drops of rain
   Came trickling down the plain.

Out it spake the king himsel,
   Ane angry man was he,
I have ane Italian within my court
   Will fight ye three and three.

Out it came that ae Italian,
   As pale as death was he;
And on the point of Johnny's sword,
   That ae Italian did die.

A clerk, a clerk, the king he cried,
   And seal her tocher wi';
A priest, a priest, lord John he cried,
   That we may married be.

For I want neither gold he said,
   Nor do I want your gear;
But I do want my ain true love,
   For I have bought her dear.

Lord Thomas of Winsberry.

It fell upon a time that the proud king of France,
    Went a hunting for five months and more,
His daughter fell in love with lord Winsberry,
    Who from Scotland was newly come o'er.
You're welcome, welcome dear father, she said,
    You are welcome again to your own,
For I have been sick, and very very sick,
    Thinking long for your coming home.

Put off your gown of green, he says,
    And spread it on yonder green,
And tell them from me that in mourning you are,
    Or that you have lain with a man.
She's put off her gown of green,
    And spread it on the strand;
Her haunches were round and her belly was big,
    From her face the colour is gone.

O is it to a man of might, he says,
    Or is it to a man that is mean;
Or is it to one of these rank rebels,
    That lately from Scotland came?
O it is to a man of might she says,
    It is not to one that is mean,
It is to Lord Thomas of Winsberry,
    And for him I must suffer pain.

The king called up his merry men all,
    By one, by two, and by three,
Go fetch me lord Thomas of Winsberry,
    Sitting under an orange tree.

Get up, get up lord Thomas, they said,
    Get up and bound your way,
For the king has sworn by his honoured crown,
    That to-morrow is thy dying day.
O what have I robb'd? or what have I stolen?
    Or what have I kill'd or slain?
That I should be afraid to speak to your king,
    For I have done him no wrong.

Lord Thomas came tripping up the stair,
    His cloathing was of the silk;
His fine yellow hair hung dangling down,
    His skin was white as the milk.
And when he came before the king,
    He kneeled down on his knee,
Says, what is your will with me my liege?
    What is your will with me?

I think no wonder, lord Thomas, he says,
    That my daughter fell in love with thee;
If thou wert a woman as thou art a man,
    My bed-fellow thou wouldst be.
Will you marry my daughter Jean?
    By the faith of my right hand,
Thou'llt have part of my gold, part of my gear,
    And a third part of my land.

Yes I will marry thy daughter Jean,
    By the faith of my right hand,
I'll have none of your gold, none of your gear,
    I have enough in fair Scotland.
He's mounted her on a milk white steed,
    Himself on a dapple grey;
He's got as much land in fair Scotland,
    As they can ride in a summer's day.

MISCELLANEOUS PIECES,
CHIEFLY ORIGINAL.

Maria; or, the Maniac's Song.—B.

A MIDNIGHT REVERIE.

(*This young woman came to Peterhead a few years ago, and has wandered about in a state of lunacy ever since.*)

STILL, I'll weave the silky garland;
Still, with roses, fond, entwine;
Still, with pearly drops bedew it;
Yet my Henry shall be mine.

But, again, this perturbation,
Foolish heart, why not at rest?
Soon thou'llt meet with adulation,
When to Henry's bosom prest.

Tears steal from these eyes, unceasing,
Briny drops new channels find;
These do quench the outward burning,
But, alas! the inward mind.

Ye who sleep on swan's down covering,
And enjoy night's sweet repose,
When you wake from silent slumber,
Pity, Oh! Maria's woes.

Think on her who nightly wanders,
Far from home,—no help-mate near;
In a land 'mong strangers, pining,
'Neath the blasts of winter drear.

Barefoot now I tread these allys,
Oft 'mong sleet, and snow, and rain;
Forc'd to rest on *granite* pillow;
For, to whom shall I complain?

Cradled in the lap of plenty,
Nurs'd by care's assiduous hand;
Pain and grief were ever strangers,
Till Henry fled to foreign land.

Once I shone with maiden graces;
Once the pride of yonder grove;
Once the hope of doating parents,
But victim now to hopeless love!

When this ring,—a parting token,
Henry gave of love, to me;
Could I think, Oh! think for ever,
I his face no more should see!

Yet it's sweet, tho' sad to look on;
Such mementos of the past
Tend to cheer the gloomy spirits,
Tho' but for a time to last.

Farewell now to all enjoyments;
Hard's my fate by all that's born;
An outcast from my friends and country;
While I wander here, forlorn!

Mary's Death.—*B.*

As the dews of the ev'ning are sweet,
   To the sun-parch'd flow'rs, a relief:
So is solitude's calm retreat,
   To a mind surcharged with grief.

The birds sit in modest dismay;
    They're mute while they perch on the thorn;
As night's sable curtain of grey
    Is tip'd with Luna's pale horn.

Yet Phœbus again shall appear,
    Again light his lamp in the east;
While Luna's shut up in the rear,
    All nature on beauties shall feast.
Return then ye choristers sweet,
    Return with joy to the grove,
'Tis there where my love and I met,
    'Tis there we unbesom'd our love.

By yon brook in the green-willow shade,
    By yon turret that mantles the sky,
My Mary first made my heart glad,
    But now she's ascended on high.
She's gone to the regions of peace,
    She's gone where mortals ne'er trod,
She's gone where the saints never cease
    To glory their infinite GOD.

Summer.—*B.*

THE sky fring'd canopy now dims
    The vast expanse of ocean's plain;
The fork'd tail'd swallow lightly skims
    The glassy face of azure main.

The laden bark, with prow erect,
　　Rises and larges in our view;
The storms are past,—escap'd the wreck,
　　And homeward bounds the jovial crew.

The sun has clos'd his western course,
　　And leaves the mountains tipt with gold;
The winding riv'lets leave their source,
　　And panting herds now seek the fold.
The lark his pious vespers close,
　　And downward plods his airy way,
To tufted grass where's mate repose,
　　There waits the light of new-born day.

When Phœbus comes on orient wings,
　　He gilds gay summer's roseate morn;
Awakes to joy, awakes and sings,
　　The little bird on blooming thorn.
Then come sweet maid unto yon shade,
　　Attended by thy flow'ry train;
And when all nature's face ye glad,
　　Keep me not one unhappy swain.

Winter.—B.

Birds forsake their leafless dwelling,
　　Sultry summer's gone and past;
Thro' yon castle-wall is swelling
　　Winter's hoarse and biting blast.

Trees are stript their native cov'ring,
  Flow'rs and foliage leave the plain;
Little birds at barndoors hov'ring,
  Anxious glean the scanty grain.

Tumbling clouds with silver tinted,
  Stretch along the 'lumin'd sky;
Nature all her works has painted,
  Pleasing to the gazer's eye.
Winter spreads her snowy mantle
  O'er each cottage, hill and dale;
Crystal trees in clusters pending;
  Timorous hares their lot bewail.

See yon bark on the vast ocean,
  By the rolling billows tost;
Up she heaves in troubled motion,
  Down again,—now to us lost!
Yet she breaks the swelling mountain,
  Spreads again the ragged sail;
Rushing thro' the foaming fountain,
  Braving dangers in the gale.

Beautiful Sue.—B.

I've wander'd all day by the stream,
  Meand'ring so limpid and gay;
Ye muses now brighten my theme!
  I sing of the daughter of May.

The hyacinth, queen of the vale,
  With flow'rets of delicate hue :—
Yet these lose their sweets, and grow pale,
  When put in the balance with Sue.

The summer, tho' rich in her bloom,
  With nature's enamelled fields,
The linnet sings sweet on the broom,
  Such pleasure this season now yields.
Some paint these in loftiest strain,
  Yet I will this fancy subdue ;
I count them but trifles —how vain,
  Compar'd with the beautiful Sue !

The violets and primrose adorn,
  And bean-flower the dew cover'd lawn ;
The lark springs to hail the new morn ;
  The sun breaking thro' the grey dawn.
The rose and the lilies give place,
  Tho' sparkling with diamonds of dew,
And yield with their splendor and dress
  The laurel to beautiful Sue.

The nectar that flows from her lip,
  A balsam for love, I am told ;
The bees crowd around her, and sip,
  To store against winter their fold
Now come ye sweet warblers, declare,
  While sporting, ye chant on the bough,
That nothing in nature's so fair
  When smiling, as beautiful Sue.

May Morning.—B.

Morning dawns, the daisey's blossom
  Hangs surcharg'd with pearly dew,
Folded in its sapphire bosom,
  Fring'd with carmine's crimson'd hue.
Blyth the sky-lark mounts on high,
  Spreading sails—his downy wings;
His magic notes rend the sky,
  Vibrissant sweetly as he sings.

Cheering Phœbus, o'er yon mountains,
  Rises heavenly to our view;
His streaming rays gild the fountains,
  And dispel the honied dew.
Planatory worlds wander,
  Far remote from haunts of men;
Purling brooks slowly meander,
  Nut-brown rivers court the main.

Summer's drest in lucid splendor,
  Decks each mountain, hill and dale;
Ambrosial fields their sweetness render
  To the zephyr's quivering gale.
Trees in robes of green are shining;
  Cowslips paint the verdant plain;
Ivy round the oak is twining,
  Variegates the ripen'd scene.

Lambkins sport in rural beauty;
  Bleating flocks their joys renew,
While they wake to love and duty,
  Bidding sable night adieu.

Hear the lutes of songsters, cheery,
    Humming o'er their matin-lay ;—
Winter's fled, no longer dreary,
    Now exchang'd for rosy MAY.

Roseate May.—B.

WHILE some with more then wonted glee
    Their ardent passions tell,
And boast all nature's charms they see
    Combin'd in Isabell.
But my soft passion to rehearse,
    I'll sing of sweeter MAY,
Tho' many far sublimer verse
    Ne'er sees the light of day.

O roseate May, queen of the year,
    Let none in anguish mourn ;
Nature her varied liveries wear,
    And hail thy sweet return.
When in thy flow'ry mantle clad,
    And robes of verdure seen,
Thou far excell'st the fairest maid
    That trips the dewey green.

Where heather blooms on highland hills ;
    Where goats climb mountains steep ;
Where trouts sport in the crystal rills ;
    And maids tend motley sheep.
These scenes, with May, would pleasant prove,
    Or Greenland's frigid coast,
As she makes summer lightly rove,
    Tho' bound with coral frost.

Cheerfu' Nancy.—B.

Rosy war her blushes, O,
Rosy war her blushes, O,
How light my heart, yet laith to part,
When met amang the bushes, O.

At e'en, by a' but heaven unseen,
  Whare modest flowers war springing, O,
Sae blythe's I've wi' my lassie been,
  While lintics they war singing, O.
    Rosy war her blushes, O,
      Rosy, &c.

We've sat beneath an ancient aik,
  Where fairies sport ilk gloaming, O,
And cushets cooing in the brake.
  Enliven'd us while roaming, O.
    Rosy war her blushes, O,
      Rosy, &c.

The birdies sung their sweetest sang,
  Down in the glen sae briery, O,
Where, hid in hazel wreaths amang,
  The mavis whistl'd cheery, O,
    Rosy war her blushes, O,
      Rosy, &c.

The wimpling burn did purling glide,
  While to yon stream retiring, O,
The troutie lav'd its sparklin' side,
  Wha could keep frae admiring, O?
    Rosy war her blushes, O,
      Rosy, &c.

K

For sports like these I min' the day,
　It lives upo' my fancy, O,
When blythe I pass'd the ev'ning grey
　Wi' my sweet cheerfu' Nancy, O.
　　Rosy war her blushes, O,
　　　Rosy, &c.

But ne'er sinsyne I seek these shades,
　They now are a' unheeded, O,
Yet ever mair I'll bless these glades,
　In love whare I succeeded, O.
　　Rosy war her blushes, O,
　　　Rosy war her blushes, O,
　　How light my heart, yet wae to part,
　　　When met amang the bushes, O.

―――

Edwin.—B.

Hark! yon waterfall how cheering,
　To the lonely musing ear!
Hark! yon low of herds, endearing,
　To the lone sequester'd pair!
Far beneath yon craggy mountain,
　Hid, unknown to public view,
See the Naiad of the fountain,
　Sweetly spread the glassy blue.

White the waters, loudly faing,
　O'er yon rock wi' roaring din;
Nature cheers the purple dawn,
　Trees o'erhang the jocund lin.

See how blythe the youthful Edwin
  Brushes thro' the pearly dews,
And the flow'ry groves of myrtle,
  To awake the nursling muse.

Sweet is she in yonder valley,
  Sweeter than the summer bloom;
Smiling like the glist'ning lily,
  Exhaling Sharon's sweet perfume.
Now this swain, with joy refreshed,
  Rises like a towering pine,
While the lovely maid's caressed,
  Shines the fairest eglantine.

Spotless Peggy.—B.

The sun danced thro' yon spreading trees,
  Where ivy twines sae finely, O.
The gurgling rill and fragrant breeze
  Invite me there sae kindly, O.
The glowing flowers and birken shade,
  And hawthorns blooming bonny, O,
Such scenes aye please the am'rous maid,
  When sporting wi' her Johnny, O.

But my delight's yon hazlie brae,
  Amang the cliffs sae craigy, O,
Where gowans spring and linties sing,
  And dwells the spotless Peggy, O

Her fleecy flock she tends wi' care,
  To fountains pure she leads them, O,
While bleating round they kiss the hand
  That daily cheers and feeds them, O.

Nae rivals there, nor crowded care,
  Shall haunt my breast sae cheery, O,
But we shall meet with transports sweet,
  When I'll embrace my deary, O.
Yestreen upo' the flowery knowe,
  Where artless birds were smiling, O,
I prest her lips of nectar'd dew,
  Nae thoughts of love beguiling, O.

Her lovely form and modest air
  Outvies the fam'd Killbeggie *, O,
And Grecian nymph was ne'er so fair,
  Nor hauf sae sweet's my Peggy, O.
In vain the artist strives to trace
  We' chisel, on the marble, O,
The sweetness of her glowing face,
  While Cupids round her warble, O.

My Mary.—B.

Dear are these shades, when Mary, blest
  I meet with thee in arbours green,
To press thy lips and angel breast,—
  That snowny breast where oft I've been.

* See the Novel of the Saxon and the Gaul.

In vain the little birds would sing;
   In vain would come the vernal year;
'Tis thou that cheer'st the infant spring;
   Without thee, all things dull appear.

More happy we where true love reigns,
   And heart for heart we there resign,
Then he who rules yon gilded plains;—
   My Mary dear, thou'rt ever mine.
Where roses blow—refreshing flowers,
   That scent the sweet and ambient gale;
Where thro' yon birks the streamlet pours,
   And soothes the lovers' am'rous tale.

To that sequestred sylvan grove,
   Let's bend our simple, artless way;
The sunny morn smiles from above,
   And choirs of songsters hail the day.
The black-bird joins his mellow note,
   And warbles sweet the vocal strain;
While roving fancy marks the spot,
   The hallow'd spot on yonder plain.

Love.—B.

Love's the soul of human blisses,
Nurs'd by fostering care, divine,
When we steal the honied kisses,
Give me love, and all is thine.

When we press the folding blossom,
Nature's masterpiece is there;
Come then to this guiless bosom,
Come, thy beauties let me share.

Come sweet rose in blushing splendour,
Rear'd 'mong wilds in simple guise;
Shun the base one's proffer'd grandeur,
Let true love obtain the prize.

For the joys can ne'er be number'd
That from lovely woman springs;
Fools 'bout factions are encumber'd,
But we dream of no such things.

Enjoyment.—B.

Altho' with submission I strove,
'Twixt honour and duty, hard by,
Till sway'd by compassionate love,
When tenderness whisper'd, reply—

I'll wed the fond girl of my heart,
For better, for worse, and thro' life;
And swore that we never should part,
So made the gay damsel my wife.

Now blest with six urchins around,
Dull time glides smoothly along;
Their prattle—more sweet is the sound
To me, than the nightingale's song.

We live in retirement, from noice,
From envy and revelry free
Each coming day brings us new joys,
Then who now so happy as we?

Generosity.—B.

Generous souls, with heavenly pity,
Mark the fate of those below;
And their mournful lorn ditty,
Throbbing with convulsive woe.

Widows, orphans, unknown merit,
Cast abroad on world wide;
Save that trickling tear,—inherit
Not a friend on earth beside.

Yet his aid with secret pleasure
Lends to those around the shrine;
And dispels in double measure
Every gloom on face that pine.

But the grov'ling sons of mammon,
Spurn poor merit's humble prayer;
And on rancour feeds each Hammon,
Till destroyed in their own snare.

Ingratitude.—B.

INGRATITUDE, thou worst of felons,
Hide, O hide thy hydra head ;
Be thou vanish'd from my dwellings,
Be exil'd from those in need !

Britons, cleave to one another ;
Like a band in concert join ;
Give then fondly to each brother,
Never let true merit pine.

Spare, O spare that sullen canker,
Ill it suits thy native grace ;
Lay aside that ruthless rancour,
Let a smile bedew the face.

Snatch that flower 'neath fortune bending,
Let it not on desert die ;
Tho' kind heaven this trial's sending,
Raising souls to soar on high.

Poverty.—B.

POVERTY, grim king of evil !
Thou that mars't domestic peace,
Hold tyrannic hand.—be civil,
From thy cruel ravage cease

Blast not joys in blooming beauty,
Flow'rs just op'ning in the bud ;
Yet thy agonizing duty
Thins life's comforts, flesh and blood.

Lank thy visage, pale and swooning :
Bleak domains and barran hills
Are thy portion, fiend of frowning,
With oppression's haggard ills.

Drear's thy melancholy grandeur,
With relentless iron bound ;
'Neath compassion's fetters wander,
Till thou givest the mortal wound.

Genius, too, alas ! seduced ;
Thou hast held them in controul,
When Pandora's box produced,
Wrings the bold aspiring soul.

Oft the generous sons of merit
Hast thou trod beneath thy feet,
While fools and cowards base, inherit,
Plenty's good, and think it meet.

The Complaint.—B.

Base the heart who thus transgresses
  Nature's law, and laws divine ;
Why was woman form'd t' oppress us ?
  Why was Nory ever mine ?

How unlike the modest gowan
    Smiling thro' the driving sleet,
When summer's verdure a' hae flow'n,
    Decks the fields baith trim and neat?

Midst the fury o' her anger,
    Winter raves wi' roaring din,
When she canna keep it langer,
    Headlong tumbles in the linn.
Yet the spring O' sweet enjoyment
    Shall return wi' double glee,
And creation's sole employment
    Glistens in the pearly ee.

But alas! to me it ever,
    E'er returns wi' double yell;
Spring nor summer, never, never,
    Cures me o'—what need I tell?
But life's winter's swiftly flying,
    Age comes wi his locks o' snaw,
When the sweetest day is dying,
    And that Nory's taen awa'.

The Storm.—B.

Frenzied waves around alarm'd us,
Above a dark and troubled sky;
Peals of light'ning show'd the mountains
Raising their white heads on high.

Earth and sea 'gainst sky combin'd ;
Thunders drove the flaming car ;
Jove and Mars—these gods entwined
To raise the elemental war.

Yet we strove against these billows,
Firm as adamantine rock ;
Masts of pine-tree crash'd as willows,
While we bore each dismal shock.

Still we labour'd, no ills brooding,
Still we wish'd the bark to save ;
But in midst of dangers, crowding,
Many found a watery grave.

In the bright phosphoric ocean,
Twinkling with the midnight blaze,
Toss'd by undulating motion,
There they cleav'd the sparkling seas.

There their beds, where many others
Sleep in briny waters, deep ;
Rock'd by Neptune, while the mothers
By lone cradles sigh and weep.

The Sheriff-muir Amazons.

Hech how, Margaret ! oman, are ye in ?
Out I am I Elspet ; an' fast did I rin,
    Down the gate to tell you,
    Down the gate to tell you,
    Down the gate to tell you,
    We'll no be left our skin !

O didna you hear? O dear, dear!
The French an' the Spaniards are a' coming here,
    An' we'll a' be murder'd,
    An' we'll a' be murder'd,
    An' we'll a' be murder'd,
    Or the neist year!

Muckle do I fear, an' sair do I doubt,
They're bringing in black Popery, fast roun' about,
    A sad reformation,
    A sad reformation,
    A sad reformation,
    In a' the kirks about!

O well kent I oman that a' wasna right,
For I dreamt o' red an' green a' the last night,
    An' twa cats fighting,
    An' twa cats fighting,
    An' twa cats fighting,
    I wauken'd in a fright!

I carena for my ain part tho' they come the morn,
I'll gie them anither link to the crooks i' the horn,
    For I'll nae yield it,
    For I'll nae yield it,
    For I'll nae yield it,
    To ony ane that's born.

O dinna ye min', o' this very fleer,
Fan we were a' rigged out to gang to Sheriff-muir,
    Wi' stanes i' our aprons,
    Wi' stanes i' our aprons,
    Wi' stanes i' our aprons,
    Did muckle diel I'm seer?

But ken ye gin neighbour Janet she be in,
An' see that ye tell her, and fast ye maun rin,
   An' auld Robie Barber,
   An' auld Robie Barber,
   An' auld Robie Barber,
   For we maun tell him.

Hech how, Margaret! wasna that a gun?
Atweel na Elspet, 'twas me braking win';
   We're well fan we get it,
   We're well fan we get it,
   We're well fan we get it,
   Awa wi' little din.

My Mantle.

Here begins this guid New Year,
   My mantle, my mantle,
Guid bless us a' that's present here,
   My Mantle's on the green hay.

Our maut-gaugers they're but loons,
   My mantle, my mantle,
They herrie the country, an' borrows towns,
   My mantle's on the green hay.

They tax the country very snell,
   My mantle, my mantle,
As they were officers frae hell,
   My mantle's on the green hay.

King James is land't at Peterhead,
    My mantle, my mantle,
An honour great to us indeed,
    My mantle on the green hay.

The night was wet and let the tide,
    My mantle, my mantle,
He couldna unto Ugie ride,
    My mantle on the green hay.

He slept a' night in our good town,
    My mantle, my mantle,
Upon a guid saft bed o' down,
    My mantle on the green hay.

In the morning when he raise,
    My mantle, my mantle,
The Marischal's bailie brush'd his claithes,
    My mantle on the green hay.

He sought neither horse nor steed,
    My mantle, my mantle,
But the auld mare carried John Reid,
    My mantle on the green hay.

He's come to set auld Scotland free,
    My mantle, my mantle,
From curs'd Hanover tyranny,
    My mantle on the green hay.

Them that does not wish him well,
    My mantle my mantle,
May highland clans wi' German steel,
    Lay their mantles on the green hay.

Mossie and his Mare.

Mossie was a cunning man,
A little Mare did buy,
For winking and for jinking
There were few could her come nigh.
She was as cunning as a fox,
As crafty as a hare,
And I will tell you by and bye
How Mossie catch'd's Mare.

Mossie on a morning
Ged out his mare to seek,
And round about the frosty bank
Upon his knees did creep;
At length he found her in a ditch,
And glad he got her there,
So put the hilter o'er her neck,
And Mossie catch'd's Mare.

Now a' ye young lasses
Whene'er ye go a wooing,
Ye may kiss and ye may clap,
But beware of evil doing,
For a dip into the honny mug
Will lead you in a snare,
And the diel will get you by the back,
As Mossie got his Mare.

And a' ye ale wives
That use there false measure,
By cheating and dissembling
For to heap up your treasure,

Cheating and dissembling
Will lead you in a snare,
And the diel will get you by the back,
As Mossie got his Mare.

And a' ye lousy tailors
That cabbage all the cloth,
Ye take a quarter from the yard,
I'm free to take my oath,
But if ye dinna mend your ways
He'll catch you in the snare,
And the diel will take you by the back
As Mossie took his Mare.

And a' ye pettyfoggers
Who plead your neighbours' cause,
The poor ye often do oppress
Against baith right and laws,
But when ye least expect it,
Hell sure will be your share,
As the diel will get you by the back,
As Mossie got his Mare.

Likewise ye whigs about the land
That deny your lawful king,
May ye be grippet in the guts,
And hung upon a string,
Lang be your corns, and short your power,
And justice get her share,
And the devil take you by the back,
As Mossie took his Mare.

The Cadgers o' Whitecrook.

It fell about the March time,
  Just i' the midst o' lent,
There came three Cadgers to Whitecrook,
  And they wou'd hae a rant:

As we're the auldest cadgers
  That live upo' the border,
We'll hae a rant into Whitecrook
  Ere we gae ony forder.

They drank frae setting o' the sun
  Until it was next dawn;
There fell a dispute them amang
  Wha wou'd pay the lawin.

They fought it out, they fought it in,
  And fought it i' the nook;
There ne'er was sic a bloody riot
  Foughten in Whitecrook.

The auld guidman got o'er the fire,
  They gied him sic a bensil,
His mou and nose gaed to the hearth;—
  Says, take ye that for hansil.

They fought it out they fought it in,
  Until they brake the cradle;
The auld guidwife sware by the laird,
  I'll riest a' your crooksaddles

And gin your saddles dinna pay
  Sic a bloody riot,
We's hae as mony fresh fish
  As be to us a diet.

L

Tawin skate upon a plate
    Aroun' their mous they wrang o't,
And a' the wives about Whitecrook,
    They did mak up a sang o't.

The auld guidwife came to the close
    The cadgers for to calm,
They dang her o'er i' the mill-led,
    Her arse closed up the dam.

She said my dancing days are done,
    Your piper plays nae well ;
Ye'll come nae mair to our town
    Wi' your Cadger's reel.

The Pipers o' Buchan.

Respectfu', renowned bagbrethren,
    Wha sells a puff wind by retail ;
Gae hearken to ane o' your kettren,—
    I in your commodity deal.
My gypsie sall try a' her cheepers,
    Her belts an' her win-breads put on,
And teen to the praise o' Scotch Pipers,
    Her chanter, reeds, burdens and drone.

Agreeable to history we're ancient,
    And honourable our pedigree ;
By Moses ye ken we are mentioned,
    Fan ilk ane had lan' that was free.
Ere aul Tubal Cain's plumb-jordon
    Had clinket a rivet upon,
Young Tubal had tun'd up his burden,
    Was liltin at 'Clout the caldron'.

Whan David was young, wi' his tykie
　　He herdit his sheep on a ley ;
At the sun-sheenie-side o' a dykie
　　The laddie first learnt to play.
Fan Saul was sere vext wi' a devil,
　　He ca'd him to play by his throne,
Auld nick got a charge o removal,
　　He scar'd him to h—ll wi' his Drone.

Fan Amphion, that famous piper,
　　Was biggin the Thebean wa',
He needit nae hewer nor cutter,
　　Nae horses the fowdrie to ca'.
For after him trees came in dances,
　　And tumble on tumble ilk stone,
Syne biggit strong ramparts and fences,
　　And a' by the sound o' his Drone.

Whan aul piper Orpheus married
　　His beautiful bride, Euridice,
By a lecherous diel she was carried
　　Straught aff to h—ll in a trice.
Th' aul piper he begg'd to restore her,
　　Wi' mony sad sigh and Ohon,
But naething the diel wad tak for her,
　　Yet tremblin, he dreadit the Drone !

Soon as his liburnims he soundit,
　　He rais'd sic an uproar in hell,
The harpies and furies confundit,
　　Broke ilka enchantment and spell.
Even Ixion's wheel wudna turn him,
　　Nor Sysiphus tumble his stone,
Sic power had his matchless liburnims,
　　Sic magical charms had his Drone.

Radamanthus and Pluto consentit
  To grant the aul piper his boon,
Proserpine sternly relentit,
  And gave him, for life, his drug-down.
He play'd Cerberus th' porter asleep,
  Then Pluto he bade him begone,
He awa wi' the carline did creep,
  And cuddom'd his wife wi' his Drone.

We are aye well loo'd by the lasses,
  In dizens and scores they'll convene,
They're sure o' maurdell o' kisses,
  Fan they get a dance o' the green.
Some cries, play us up 'Sleepy Maggy',
  'Tail Toddle,' or 'Nancy does you;'
And some seeks the 'Best o' the Baggie',
  And dances like daft to our Drone.

Ye'll hear the young wenches conferrin
  Wi' aul auntie Bess at their wheel,
Their joes and their sweet-hearts comparin,
  And wha has the lover maist leal.
Quo Jeannie, I like my dear Jamie,
  (But telling this secret to none,)
For ilka time he comes to see me,
  I aye get a spring on his Drone.

Quo Nelly, my piper's my jewel,
  Luve burns at my heart like a coal,
Sae neatly he handles the tewel,
  His fingers sae sweet on the hole.
Its happiness to me to hear him
  'Play o'er the green meadows alone',
But Oh I am blest whan I'm near him,
  Whan o'er my lap he lays his Drone!

Quo Betty, I mean not to tarry,
    For I've made a promise and vow,
My piper, my sodger, I'll marry,
    For I like the red and the blue.
Then I'll get the knapsack to carry,
    Sae merrily as we'll march on;
There's naething like the military,
    To follow the drum and the Drone

Hear me, says aul Bessie, their auntie,
    I've liv'd wi' my piper, its true,
O' simmers and winters these twenty,
    And never had cause yet to rue.
He's well-worth his room in the pantry,
    He ne'er gae me reason to moan,
He's fed me fu' well wi' his chauntrie,
    And gard me gie braw wi' his Drone.

We are honest in our occupation,
    It lies na in our way to cheat,
It's 'gainst the laws o' our profession
    To seek ony mair than we get.
But gin ony gen'rous fellows
    Their bountith bestow us upon,
Our gratitude blows like our bellows,
    We soun forth their praise wi' our Drone.

We deavna the house wi' state-matters,
    Whan we're at our pint or our gill,
But wha best pinches and barters,
    And wha o' reed-makin has skill.
We fashna our head wi' the banters
    Tweesh Prelate and Presbyter John,
But buyin and nifferin o' chanters,
    And teenin, and soundin our Drone.

Our lug and our finger exact is,
   To measure our time and our rest,
The theory wantin the practice,
   Is stark-staring nonesence at best.
Our thumb has the knack o' transposing,
   Or shifting o' the semitone,
We play to the key at the closing,
   And symphony souns wi' our Drone.

Our brave highlan heroes it charms,
   When their martial pibrochs they hear,
Their matchless atchievements in arms,
   Keeps a' the wide warld in fear.
How mony strong forts hae they storm'd,
   How mony fierce battles they've won,
What wonders hae they not perform'd,
   Inspir'd by the soun o' the Drone?

Now join in a toast to Scotch pipers,
   A piper, you see, is a knabb,
Come then lat us teen up our cheepers,
   Our honour swells up like our bag.
Our company's welcome to princes,
   By the rangel we're doated upon,
For gladness their verra heart dances,
   To hear the sweet chanter and Drone.

Lord and Lady Errol.

O Errol's place is a bonny place,
   It stands upon yon plain,
The flowers on it grow red and white,
   The apples red and green.

CHORUS.
The ranting o't, and the danting o't,
 According as ye ken,
The thing they ca' the danting o't,
 Lady Errol lies her lane!

O Errol's place is a bonny place,
 It stands upon yon plain,
But what's the use of Errol's place,
 He's no like other men?
  The ranting, &c.

As I cam in by yon canal,
 And by yon bowling green,
I might hae pleased the best Carnegy
 That ever bore that name.
  The ranting, &c

As sure's your name is Kate Carnegy,
 And mine is Gibbie Hay,
I'll gar your father sell his land,
 Your tocher for to pay.
  The ranting, &c.

To gar my father sell his land,
 Would it not be a sin,
To give it to a naughtless lord,
 That couldna get a son?
  The ranting, &c.

Now she is on to to Edinburgh
 For to try the law,
And Errol he has followed her
 His manhood for to shaw.
  The ranting, &c.

Then out it spake her sister,
    Whose name was lady Jane,
Had I been lady Errol, she says,
    Or come of sic a clan,
I would not in this public way,
    Have sham'd my own gudeman.
        The ranting, &c.

But Errol got it in his will
    To choice a maid himsel,
And he has taen a country girl
    Came in her milk to sell.
        The ranting, &c.

He took her by the milk-white hand,
    And led her up the green,
And twenty times he kiss'd her there
    Before his lady's een.
        The ranting, &c.

He took her by the milk white hand,
    And led her up the stair,
Says, thrice three hundred pounds I'll gie
    To you, to bear an heir.
        The ranting, &c.

He kept her there into a room
    Three quarters of a year.
And when the three quarters were out,
    A braw young son she bear.
        The ranting, &c.

Tak hame your daughter, Carnegy,
    And put her till a man,
For Errol he cannot please her,
    Nor any of his men.
        The ranting, &c.

Lord Salton and Auchanachie.

Ben cam her father, skipping on the floor,
  Said Jeanie, your trying the tricks of a whore.
Your caring for him that cares not for thee,
  And I pray you take Salton, let Auchanachie be.
I will not have Salton, it lies low by the sea:
  He is bowed in the back, he's thrawen in the knee
And I'll die if I get not my brave Auchanachie.

I am bowed in the back, lassie as ye see,
  But the bonny lands of Salton are no crooked tee.
And when she was married, she would not lie down,
  But they took out a knife and cuttit her gown:

Likewies of her stays, the lacing in three,
  And now she lies dead for her dear Auchanachie
Out comes her bower woman wringing her hands,
  Says, alas! for the staying so long on the sands.
Alas! for the staying so long on the flood,
For Jeanie was married, and now she is dead!

'Bonny John Seton.

Upon the eighteenth day of June
  A dreary day to see,
The Southern lords did pitch their camp
  Just at the bridge of Dee.

Bonny John Seton of Pitmeddin,
   A bold baron was he,
He made his testament ere he went out,
   The wiser man was he.

He left his land to his young son,
   His lady her dowry,
A thousand crowns to his daughter Jean,
   Yet on the nurse's knee.

Then out came his lady fair,
   A tear into her e'e,
Says, stay at home, my own good lord,
   O stay at home with me!

He looked over his left shoulder,
   Cried, soldiers follow me!
O then she looked in his face,
   An angry woman was she;
God send me back my steed again,
   But ne'er let me see thee.

His name was Major Middleton,
   That manned the bridge of Dee;
His name was Colonel Henderson,
   That let the cannons flee.

His name was Major Middleton,
   That manned the bridge of Dee,
And his name was Colonel Henderson,
   That dung Pitmeddin in three.

Some rode on the black and grey,
   And some rode on the brown;
But the bonny John Seton,
   Lay gasping on the ground.

Then by there comes a false Forbes,
    Was riding from Driminere,
Says, here there lies a proud Seton,
    This day they ride the rear.

Craigievar said to his men,
    You may play on your shield,
For the proudest Seton in all the lan,
    This day lies on the field.

O spoil him, spoil him, cried Craigievar,
    Him spoiled let me see,
For on my word, said Craigievar,
    He had no good will at me.

They took from him his armour clear,
    His sword, likewise his shield;
Yea, they have left him naked there,
    Upon the open field.

The highland men they're clever men,
    At handling sword and shield,
But yet they are too naked men,
    To stay in battle field.

The highland men are clever men,
    At handling sword or gun,
But yet they are too naked men,
    To bear the cannon's rung.

For a cannon's roar in a summer night,
    Is like thunder in the air,
There's not a man in highland dress,
    Can face the cannon's fire.

Mary Hamilton.

Then down cam Queen Marie,
   Wi' goud links in her hair,
Saying, Marie mild, where is the child,
   That I heard greet sae sair?

There was nae child wi' me madam,
   There was nae child wi' me,
It was but me in a sair cholic,
   When I was like to die!

I'm not deceived, Queen Marie said,
   No, no, indeed! not I!
So Marie mild, where is the child?
   For sure I heard it cry.

She turned down the blankets fine,
   Likewise the Holland sheet,
And underneath there strangled lay,
   A lovely baby sweet.

O cruel mother! said the Queen,
   Some fiend possessed thee,
But I will hang thee for this deed,
   My Marie tho' thou be!

When she cam to the Netherbow-port,
   She laught loud laughters three;
But when she cam to the gallows foot,
   The salt tear blinded her e'e.

Yestreen the Queen had four Maries,
   The night she'll hae but three;
There was Marie Seton, and Marie Beaton,
   And Marie Carmichael and me.

Ye mariners, ye mariners,
  That sail upon the sea,
Let not my father or mother wit,
  The death that I maun die.

I was my parents' only hope,
  They ne'er had ane but me,
They little thought when I left hame,
  They should nae mair me see!

The Burning of Frendraught-House.

The eighteenth day of October,
  A dismal tale to hear
How good lord John and Rothiemay,
  Were both burnt in the fire.

When steeds were saddled and well bridled,
  And ready for to ride,
Then out there came the false Frendraught,
  Inviting them to bide.

Said stay this night until we sup,
  The morn until we dine,
'Twill be a token of good 'greement,
  'Twixt your good lord and mine.

We'll turn again, said good lord John,
  But, no! said Rothiemay,
My steed's trapanned, my bridle's broken,
  I fear the day I'm fay.

When mass was sung, and bells were rung,
    And all men bound for bed,
Then good lord John and Rothiemay,
    In one chamber were laid.

They had not long cast off their clothes,
    And were but new asleep,
When weary smoke began to rise,
    Likewise the scorching heat.

O waken, waken, Rothiemay,
    O waken, brother dear,
And turn you to your Saviour,
    There is strong treason here.

When they were dressed wi' their clothes,
    And ready for to boun',
The doors and windows were secured,
    The roof-tree burning down.

He did flee to the wire window,
    As fast as he could gang,
Says, woe to the hands put in the staunchions,
    For out we'll never win.

While he stood at the wire window,
    Most doleful to be seen,
He did espy the lady Frendraught,
    Who stood upon the green.

Mercy, mercy, lady Frendraught!
    Will ye not sink with sin?
For first your husband kill'd my father,
    And now you burn his son.

O then out spake the lady Frendraught,
 And loudly did she cry;
It were great pity for good lord John,
 But none for Rothiemay:
The keys were casten in the deep draw well,
 Ye cannot win away.

While he stood in this dreadful plight,
 Most piteous to be seen,
Then called out his servant Gordon,
 As he had frantic been.

O loup, O loup my dear master!
 O loup and come to me,
I'll catch you in my arms two,
 One foot I will not flee.

O loup, O loup, my dear master!
 O loup and come away,
I'll catch you in my arms two,
 But Rothiemay may lay.

The fish shall ne'er swim in the flood,
 Nor corn grow thro' the clay,
Nor the fiercest fire that e'er was kindled,
 Twin me and Rothiemay.

I cannot loup, I cannot come,
 I cannot win to thee,
My head's fast in the wire window,
 My feet burning from me.

My eyes are southering in my head,
 My flesh roasting also,
My bowels are boiling with my blood,
 Is not that a woeful woe?

Take here the rings from my white fingers,
   Which are so long and small,
And give them to my lady fair,
   Where she sits in her hall.

I cannot loup, I cannot come,
   I cannot loup to thee,
My earthly part is all consum'd,
   My spirit speaks to thee.

Wringing her hands, tearing her hair,
   His lady fair was seen,
Calling unto his servant Gordon,
   Where he stood on the green.

O woe be to you George Gordon,
   An ill death may you dee,
So safe and sound as ye stand there,
   And my lord burned from me.

I bade him loup, I bade him come,
   I bade him come to me;
I'd catch him in my arms two,
   A foot I would not flee.

He threw me the rings from his white fingers,
   Which were so long and small,
To give to you, his lady fair,
   Where you sit in your hall.

Sophia Hay, Sophia Hay,
   Bonny Sophia was her name;
Her waiting maid put on her clothes,
   But she tore them off again.

And oft she cried, Ohon, alas!
A sair heart is easy wan,
I wan a sair heart when I married him,
The day its returned again.

Frennet Hall.

(THE MODERN WAY OF FRENDRAUGHT.)

When Frennet Castle's ivied walls
 Thro' yallow leaves were seen;
When birds forsook the sapless boughs,
 And bees the faded green;

Then lady Frennet, vengeful dame,
 Did wander frae the ha',
To the wild forest's dewie gloom,
 Amang the leaves that fa'.

Her page, the swiftest of her train,
 Had clumb a lofty tree,
Whose branches to the angry blast
 Were soughing mournfullie.

He turn'd his een towards the path,
 That near the castle lay,
Where good lord John and Rothiemay,
 Were riding down the brae.

Swift darts the eagle from the sky,
 When prey beneath is seen,
As quickly he forgot his hold,
 And perch'd upon the green.

M

O hie thee, hie thee, lady gay,
  Frae this dark wood awa,
Some visitors of gallant mein,
  Are hasting to the ha'.

Then round she row'd her silken plaid,
  Her feet she didna spare,
Until she left the forest skirts,
  A lang bow-shot and mair.

O where, O where, my good lord John,
  O tell me where you ride?
Within my castle-wall this night,
  I hope you mean to bide.

Kind nobles, will ye but alight,
  In yonder bower to stay?
Saft ease shall teach you to forget
  The hardness of the way.

Forbear entreaty, gentle dame,
  How can we here remain?
Full well you ken your husband dear
  Was by our father slain.

The thoughts of which, with fell revenge.
  Your angry bosom swell:
Enrag'd you've sworn that blood for blood
  Should this black passion quell.

O fear not, fear not, good lord John,
  That I will you betray,
Or sue requital for a debt,
  Which nature cannot pay.

Bear witness, a' ye powers on high,
　Ye lights that gin to shine,
This night shall prove the sacred cord,
　That knits your faith and mine.

The lady slee, with honeyed words,
　Entic'd thir youths to stay;
But morning sun ne'er shone upon
　Lord John nor Rothiemay.

Lady Keith's Consolation.

I may sit in my wee croo house,
　At the rock and the reel to toil fu' dreary;
I may think on the day that's gane,
　And sigh and sab till I grow weary.
I ne'er could brook, I ne'er could brook,
　A foreign loon to own or flatter;
But I will sing a ranting sang,
　The day our king comes o'er the water.

O gin I live to see the day,
　That I hae begg'd, and begg'd frae Heaven,
I'll fling my rock and reel away,
　And dance and sing frae morn till even:
For there is ane I winna name,
　That comes the beingin bike to scatter;
And I'll put on my bridal gown,
　That day our king comes o'er the water.

I hae seen the gude auld day,
    The day o' pride and chieftain glory,
When royal Stuarts bare the sway,
    And ne'er heard tell o' Whig nor Tory.
Though lyart be my locks and grey,
    And eild has crook'd me down—what matter;
I'll dance and sing ae ither day,
    That day our king comes o'er the water.

A curse on dull and drawling Whig,
    The whining, ranting, low deceiver,
Wi' heart sae black, and look sae big,
    And canting tongue o' clishmaclaver!
My father was a good lord's son,
    My mother was an earl's daughter,
And I'll be lady Keith again,
    That day our king comes o'er the water.

Nae Dominies for me, Laddie.

As I went forth to take the air,
    Into an evening clear, laddie
I met a brisk young handsome spark,
    A new-made pulpitier, laddie:
An airy blade so brisk and bra,
    Mine eyes did never see, laddie;
A long cravat at him did wag,
    His hose girt 'boon the knee, laddie.

By and out o'er this young man had,
    A gallant douse black gown, laddie,
With cock'd up hat, and powder'd wig,
    Black coat, and muffs fu' clean, laddie.

At length he did approach me nigh,
    And bowing down full low, laddie ;
He grasp'd me, as I did pass by,
    And would not let me go, laddie.

Said I. pray, friend, what do you mean ?
    Canst thou not let me be, laddie ?
Says he, my heart, by Cupid's dart,
    Is captive unto thee, lassie.
I'll rather chuse to thole grim death :
    So cease and let me be, laddie.
For what ? said he.—Good troth, said she,
    Nae dominies for me, laddie.

Ministers' stipends are uncertain rents
    For ladies' conjunct fee, laddie ;
When books and gowns are all cry'd down,
    Nae dominies for me, laddie.
But for your sake I'll fleece the flock,
    Grow rich as I grow auld, lassie ;
If I be spar'd, I'll be a laird,
    And thou be Madam call'd, lassie.

But what if ye should chance to die,
    Leave bairns ane or twa, laddie ?
Naething would be reserv'd for them,
    But hair-mould books to gnaw, laddie.
At this he angry was, I wat,
    He gloom'd and lock'd fu' hie, laddie ;
When I perceived this, in haste
    I left my dominie, laddie.

Then I went hame to my step-dame,
    By this time it was late, laddie ;
But she before had barr'd the door,
    I blush'd and look'd fu' blate, laddie.

Thinks I, I must ly in the street,
  Is there no room for me, laddie;
And is their neither plaid nor sheet
  With my young dominie, laddie?

Then with a humble voice, I cry'd,
  Pray open the door to me, laddie:
But he reply'd, I'm gone to bed,
  So cease, and let me be, lassie.
The sooner that you let me in,
  You'll be the more at ease, laddie;
And on the morrow I'll be gone,
  Then marry whom you please, laddie.

And what if I should chance to die,
  Leave bairns ane or twa, lassie,
Naething would be reser'd for them,
  But hair-mould books to gnaw, lassie.
Ministers' stipends are uncertain rents
  For ladies' conjunct-fee, lassie;
When books and gowns are a' cry'd down,
  Nae dominies for me, lassie.

So fare you well, my charming maid,
  This lesson learn of me, lassie,
At the next offer hold him fast,
  That first makes love to thee, lassie.
Then I did curse my doleful fate,
  Gin this had been my lot, laddie,
For to have match'd with such as you,
  A good-for-nothing sot, laddie.

Then I returned hame again,
  And coming down the town, laddie,
By my good luck I chanc'd to meet
  A gentleman dragoon, laddie:

And he took me by baith the hands,
  'Twas help in time of need, laddie;
Fools on ceremonies stand,
  At twa words we agreed, laddie.

He led me to his quarter-house,
  Where we exchang'd a word, laddie;
We had nae use for black gowns there,
  We married o'er the sword, laddie.
Martial drums is music fine,
  Compar'd wi' tinkling bells, laddie;
Gold, red, and blue, is more divine
  Than black, the hue of hell, laddie.

Kings, queens, and princes, crave the aid
  Of the brave stout dragoons, laddie;
While dominies are much employ'd
  'Bout whores and sackcloth gowns, laddie.
Awa' then wi' these whining lowns,
  They look like let me be, laddie;
I've mair delight in roaring guns:
  Nae dominies for me, laddie.

Logie o' Buchan.

O Logie o' Buchan, O Logie the laird,
They hae taen awa Jamie that delv'd in the yard,
Wha play'd on the pipe an' the viol sae sma;
They hae taen awa Jamie the flower o' them a'.
  He said, Think na lang, lassie, tho' I gang awa,
  He said, Think na lang, lassie, tho' I gang awa;
  For the simmer is coming, cauld winter's awa,
  And I'll come and see thee in spite o' them a',

O Sandy has owsen, has gear, and has kye,
A house and a haddin, and siller forbye,
But I wad hae Jamie wi's staff in his hand,
Before I'd hae Sandy wi's houses and land.
  He said, &c.

My daddy looks sulky, my minny looks sour,
They frown upon Jamie because he is poor;
But daddy and minny, altho' that they be,
There,s nane o' them a' like my Jamie to me.
  He said, &c.

I sit on my creepie, and spin at my wheel,
And think on the laddie that loved me sae weel;
He had but ae saxpence, and brak it in twa,
And gied me the hauf o't when he gaed awa.
  Then haste ye back, Jamie, and bide na awa,
  Then haste ye back, Jamie, and bide na awa;
  Simmer is coming, cauld winter's awa,
  And ye'll come and see me in spite o' them a'.

By the side of a country kirk wall.

By the side of a country kirk wall,
 A sullen Whig minister stood,
Enclos'd in an old oaken stall,
 Apart from the rest of the crowd.
His hat was hung high on a pin,
 With the cocks so devoutly display'd;
And the cloak that conceal'd ev'ry sin
 On the pulpit was carefully spread.

In pews and in benches below
  The people were variously plac'd ;
Some attentively gaz'd at the show,
  Some loll'd like blythe friends at a feast.
With a volley of coughs and of sighs,
  A harsh noisy murmur was made,
While Pitney threw up both his eyes,
  And thus he began to his trade :

My dearly beloved, quoth he,
  Our religion is now at a stand ;
The Pretender's come over the sea,
  And his troops are disturbing our land.
The Papists will sing their old song,
  And burn all our Bibles with fire,
And we shall be banish'd ere long ;
  'Tis all that the Tories desire.

They'll tell you he's Protestant bred,
  And he'll guard your religion and laws ;
But, believe me, whate'er may be said,
  He's a foe to the Whigs and their cause.
May thick darkness, as black as the night,
  Surround each rebellious pate !
And confusion to all that will fight
  In defence of the dastardly brat.

Our kirks, which we've long time enjoy'd,
  Will be fill'd with dull rogues in their gowns,
And our stipends will then be employ'd
  On fellows that treat us like clowns.
Their bishops, their deans, and the rest
  Of the pope's antichristian crew
Will be then of our livings possest,
  And they'll lord it o'er us and o'er you.

Instead of a sleep in your pews,
    You'll be vex'd with repeating the creed;
You'll be dumn'd and demur'd with their news,
    If this their damn'd project succeed.
Their mass and their set forms of prayer
    Will then in our pulpits take place:
We must kneel till our breeches are bare,
    And stand at the glore and the grace.

Let us rise like true Whigs in a band,
    As our fathers have oft done before,
And slay all the Tories off hand,
    And we shall be quiet once more.
But before he accomplish his hopes,
    May the thunder and lightning come down;
And tho' Cope could not vanquish his troops,
    May the clouds keep him back from the throne!

Thus when he had ended his task,
    With the sigh of a heavenly tone,
The precenter got up in his desk,
    And sounded his musical drone.
Now the hat is taen down from the pin,
    And the cloak o'er the shoulders is cast;
The people throng out with a din,
    The devil take him that is last!

Charly now that's o'er the sea.—B.

    Charly now is o'er the sea,
    Charly now is o'er the sea,
    Wha will now us comfort gie,
    Sin Charly he gaed o'er the sea?

He'll roam nae mair 'mang heather bells,
O'er mountains blue, and purple vales,
Nor breathe the fragrance o' our gales,
   Sin Charly he gaed o'er the sea.
   Charly now that's, &c.

Tho' mony thought the cause was bad,
What cou'd we do but help the lad,
Whan dress'd in's plaid and Scotch cockade,
   Charly now that's o'er the sea?
   Charly now that's, &c.

He lik'd our glens and tow'ring hills,
Our browsing flocks, and gurgling rills,
Our hearts o' steel to right his ills;
   Charly now that's o'er the sea.
   Charly now that's, &c.

But may his joys be e'er complete,
His en'mies crush'd beneath his feet,
Until kind fortune think it meet
   To change his fate that's o'er the sea.
   Charly now that's, &c,

Tho' some folks blam'd him right severe,
And hauntit him unto the snare,
Which drave him wildly to despair,
   And put our Charly o'er the sea.
   Charly now that's, &c.

Yet shall ilk honour crown his brow,
Tho' distant far from's mountains blue,
Nor stain the kilt and bonnet true,
   O' Charly that is o'er the sea.
   Charly now that's, &c.

Adam o' Gordon.

It fell about the Martinmass,
    Qhen the wind blew shril and cauld,
Said Adam o' Gordon to his men,
    We maun draw to a hauld.

And what an a hauld sall we draw to,
    My mirry men and me?
We will gae strait to Towie-house,
    To see that fair ladie.

The lady on her castle wa'
    Beheld baith dale and donn,
When she was 'ware of a host of men
    Riding toward the toun.

O see ze not my mirry men a',
    O see ze not what I see?
Methinks I see an host of men.
    I marvel what they be.

She wein'd it had been her luvely lord,
    As he came riding hame;
It was the traitor Adam o' Gordon,
    Wha reck'd nae sin or shame.

She had nae sooner busket hersel,
    Nor putten on her gown,
Till Adam o' Gordon, and his men,
    Were round about the town.

They had nae sooner sitten down,
    Nor sooner said the grace,
Till Adam o' Gordon, and his men,
    Were closed about the place.

The lady ran up to her tower-head,
　As fast as she could drie,
To see, if by her fair speeches,
　She could with him agree.

As soon as he saw the lady fair,
　And hir yates all locked fast,
He fell into a rage of wrath,
　And his heart was aghast.

Cum doun to me, ze lady fair,
　Cum doun to me, let's see,
This night ze's ly by my ain side,
　The morn my bride sall be.

I winnae cum doun, ye false Gordon,
　I winnae cum doun to thee,
I winnae forsake my ain dear lord,
　That is sae far frae me.

Gi up your house, ze fair ladye,
　Gi up your house to me,
Or I will burn zoursell therein,
　Bot, and zour babies three.

I winnae gie up, zou fals Gordon,
　To nae sik traitor as thee,
Tho' zou should burn mysell therein,
　Bot, and my babies three.

But reach me my pistol, Glaud my man,
　And charge ze weil my gun,
For, bot if I pierce that bluidy butcher,
　We a' sall be undone.

She stude upon the castle wa'
    And let twa bullets flie;
She mist that bluidy butcher's heart,
    And only raz'd his knie.

Set fire to the house, quoth fals Gordon,
    Sin better may nae be;
And I will burn hersel therein,
    Bot, and her babies three.

And ein wae worth ze, Jock, my man,
    I paid zou weil zour fee,
Why pou ze out my ground wa' stane,
    Lets in the reek to me?

And ein wae worth ze, Jock, my man,
    For I paid zou well your hire;
Why pou ze out my ground wa' stane,
    To me lets in the fire?

Ze paid me weil my hire, ladye,
    Ze paid me weil my fee;
But now I'm Adam o' Gordon's man,
    Maun either do or die.

O then bespake her zoungest son,
    Sat on the nurse's knee,
Dear mother, gie owre zour house, he says,
    For the reek it worries me.

I winnae gie up my house, my dear,
    To nae sik traitor as he;
Cum weil, cum wae, my jewels fair,
    Ze maun tak share wi' me.

But I wad gie my gowd, my chyld,
　　Sae wald I a' my fee,
For ae blast o' the westlin wind,
　　To blaw the reik frae thee.

O then bespake her dochter dear,
　　She was baith jimp and sma',
O row me in a pair o' sheets,
　　And tow me owre the wa'.

They row'd her in a pair o sheets,
　　And tow'd her owre the wa',
But on the point o' Gordon's speir
　　She gat a deadly fa'.

O bonnie, bonnie was her mouth,
　　And chirry was her cheiks;
And cleir, cleir was hir yallow hair,
　　Wharon the reid bluid dreips!

Then wi' his speir he turn'd her owre—
　　O gin hir face was wan!
Quoth he, Ze are the first that eir
　　I wish'd alive again.

He turn'd her owre and owre again—
　　O gin her skin was white!
I micht hae spar'd that bonny face,
　　To hae been some man's delyte.

Busk and boun, my mirry men a',
　　For ill doom do I guess:
I canno luik on that bonny face,
　　As it lyes on the grass.

Wha luik to freits, my master deir,
　　Freits will aye follow them:
Let it neir be said, Adam o' Gordon
　　Was daunted by a dame.

But when the lady saw the fire
    Cum flaming owr her head,
She weip'd and kist her children twain,
    My bairns we been but deid.

The Gordon then his bugil blew,
    And said, awa, awa;
Sin Towie-House is a' in flame,
    I had it time to ga.

O then bespied her ain deir lord,
    As he cam owr the lee;
He saw his castle in a blaze,
    Sae far as he could see.

Then sair, O sair, his mind misgave,
    And a' his heart was wae;
Put on, put on my wichty men,
    Sae fast as ze can gae.

Put on, put on, my wichty men,
    Sae fast as ze can drie;
He that is hindmost o' the thrang,
    Sall neir get gude o' me.

Then sum they rade, and sum they ran,
    Fu fast outowre the bent,
But ere the foremost could win up,
    Baith lady and babes were brint.

He wrang his hands, he rent his hair,
    And weipt in teinfu mude:
Ah traitors, for this cruel deid,
    Ye sall weip teirs o' bluid!

And after the Gordon he has gane,
    Sae fast as he micht drie:
And sune in his foul hartis bluid,
    He has wrekin his deir ladie.

EXPLANATORY NOTES.

Sir James the Rose, (old way.)

This tragical ballad has been written at a very early period, and proves that there have been Delilahs in Scotland in the days of Sir James the Rose, as well as in the land of Timnath in the days of Samson, who for a small meid, would sacrifice their dearer half to the satifaction of their blood-thirsty enemies: but the consequence is, that the wages of unrighteousness never prosper in their hand: for,

    She wander'd to the dowie glen,
    And nevir mair was sein!

Sir James the Rose, (modern way.)

This is one of the most beautiful ballads that I know. It is also called the Buchanshire Tragedy, and said to have been written by Michael Bruce, a young man of great poetical abilities, who died in a consumption in the 21st year of his age. A copy of this ballad appeared in the Annual Register in the year 1776, which, with the copy in his own poems, differ considerably from every other that I have seen, and some even prior to the earliest edition of his works. In an old collection of ballads, I have found one called Elfrida and Sir James of Perth, which resemble it very much; and, I have every reason to think it is the older of the two, although they both include in their historical part, some of the circumstances that befall the heroes of the poems at the memorable battle of Flodden-field, where Scotland lost her king and the flower of her nobility.

At the Abbey of Deer, about ten miles from Peterhead, is still pointed out to the curious, the trysting thorn; or, in other words, the blooming saugh-tree on the bank of the burn, where these youthful lovers, the brave Sir James the Rose, and and Matilda, lord Buchan's beautiful daughter, were wont to meet to tell their tender tales.

Alcanzor and Zaida.

This pathetic tale is Moorish, imitated from the Spanish by Percy.

The Lake of the dismal Swamp.

In this American ballad, the effects of love is finely pourtrayed in the mind of a young man who lost his senses upon the death of a girl he loved, and who, suddenly disappearing from his friends, was never afterwards heard of. As he had frequently said in his ravings, that the girl was not dead, but gone to the Dismal Swamp, it is supposed he had wandered into that dreary wilderness, and had died of hunger, or been lost in some of its dreadful morasses.

The Great Dismal Swamp is 10 or 12 miles distant from Norfolk, and the Lake in the middle of it, (about 7 miles long) is called Drummond's Pond.

Bryan and Pereene.

This West-Indian ballad was written by Dr. James Granger, and founded on a real fact that happened in the Island of St. Christopher.

Young Gregor's Ghost.

In the early part of the American wars, when our brave highland countrymen volunteered their services to cross the Western Ocean, to claim and maintain the rights of their country, Young Gregor, loved Gregor, was torn from the bosom of all his earthly happiness, the bosom of his sweet Katty Macfarlane. Gregor's father, at one time, was very affluent, and had taught his son the usual branches of education, with the addition of Latin and French; but owing to him being engaged in the rebellion of 1745—6, he was obliged to leave his native country and seek shelter from the fury of his pursuers in the wilds and fastnesses of Columbia, where he breathed his last. The young man was entrusted to the care of his uncle, who proved his ruin, by causing him to be kidnapped by a band of soldiers and sent away, where he was killed by the savage Indians near Fort Niagara, on the 30th July, 1759.

The sequel of the ballad is touchingly pathetic, —His spirit returns—meets his love beneath the green oak tree—shows her his bleeding wounds— she goes to embrace him, but in an instant he is vanished, and vanished for ever, leaving her a sad and disconsolate prey to the cruelty of a hardened and unrelenting father!

The Jew's Daughter.

In the dark ages the prejudices against the Jews gave rise to many stories of their cruelties to Christians, which were fostered by the priests, and believed by the people. The subject on which this ballad is founded, is a supposed murder committed by the Jews at Lincoln on a boy, in the reign of Henry III. While amusing himself at an innocent pastime with other youths, near a Jew's house, Sir Hugh strikes the ball through the window; he solicites the Jew's daughter to throw it back to him, but she refuses, and endeavours to entice him into the house, which he at last enters; when in her power, she puts him to death, and to conceal her guilt, throws his body into a deep well; his mother makes every search for him, and in her lamentation invokes his spirit to tell her where he is laid; the poet here calls to his aid the superstition of the times, makes the boy answer his mother from the bottom of the well, meet her at an appointed place, and sets the bells a-ringing withount human aid. Miracles such as these were not only current, but implicitly believed, and even at this day not discredited.

Cruel Lammikin.

This ballad is undoubtedly very old, and appears to have had some foundation in truth.

The Faithless Captain.

In this ballad is shown one of the many fatal effects that follow seduction. The heroine of this lamentable ballad was waiting-maid to an aged lady in London, whose son commanded the Burford, an East-India trader. This young seaman unsuspectingly stole the heart of his mother's maid; who, after having made many oaths and protestations to her of his love and constancy, he left her to mourn her lost honour, and his perjured vows. She, however, found means to get herself dressed in man's attire, and entered herself on board of the Burford, unknown to the Captain. After having been sometime at sea, he discovered the trick, when they were married, and shortime afterward made their bed in each other's arms in the watery deep.

The Gosport Tragedy.

How many stratagems does the devil invent to decoy and ensnare poor unsuspecting females? And how oft is the tender heart of the modest maiden made to shed tears of blood by the savage oppression of cruel and tyranical man? Molly, once the beauty of Gosport, was inhumanly butchered for too implicitly placing her affections on one of these ungrateful, and blood-thirsty cannibals.—The consequence however was, as is always the case, the murderer met with his due reward.

Rosanna's Overthrow.

Who would believe the wretchedness of human nature, or the evil inventions of man, to rob the innocent and fairer part of the creation of all that they hold dear in this world—life and honour? This ballad is similar to the preceding; a young man under fair pretences gains the affections of a knight's daughter in Oxfordshire, whom, after having seduced, he murdered.

Fair Rosamond.

Most of the circumstances in this popular story of Henry II. and the beautiful Rosamond, have been believed by our historians; who, unable to account for the unnatural conduct of Queen Eleanor in stimulating her sons to rebellion, have attributed it to jealousy, and supposed that Henry's amour with Rosamond was the object of that passion.

Stowe describes it to be "a house of wonderful working; so that no man or woman might come to her, but he that was instructed by the king, or such as were right secret with touching the matter. This house after sometime was named Labyrinthus, or Dedalus worke. which was wrought like unto a knot in a garden, called a maze."

Historians differ as to the manner by which the Queen gained admittance to Rosamond's bower. Hollingshed says, "that the Queen found her out by a silken thread, which the King had drawn after him out of his chamber with his foot, and dealt with her in such shape and cruel wise, that she lived not long after."--On the contrary, Speede tells us that the jealous Queen found her out "by a clew of silk fallen from Rosamond's lappe, as shee sate to take ayre, and fleeing from the sight of the scarcher, the end of her silk thread fastened to her foot, and the clew unwinding, remained behinde: which the Queene followed, till she had found what she sought, and upon Rosamond so vented her spleene, as the lady lived not long after."

The death of Rosamond by poison, is doubtful. None of the old writers attribute it to that cause. (Stowe, indeed, mentions it as a slight conjecture.) They only give us to understand, that the Queen treated her harshly, which probably had such an effect on her spirits, that she did not long survive it. She died in 1177. Rosamond's father (Walter lord Clifford,) having been a great benefactor to the nunnery at Godstow, where she had also resided in the innocent part of her life, her body was conveyed there, and buried in the middle part of the choir, in which place it remained till the year 1191, when Hugh, bishop of Lincoln ordered it to be removed.

Henry had two sons by Rosamond, William Longue-espe, earl of Salisbury, and Geoffrey, bishop of Lincoln.

The Death of Leith-Hall.

This tragedy was acted in Aberdeen at Martinmass 1763, in the house of Archibald Campbell, Vintner, Castle-Street, but a few years ago. The ball that gave the mortal wound to Leith-Hall, was seen sticking in one of the lamp-posts of that place. I had this copy from a respectable tradesman's wife who recollects the circumstance.

The Baron of Braikley.

There are various copies of this ballad to be met with among the antiquarians, which differ considerably from the one here inserted; but I hold this to be among the best. The hero of the poem is John Gordon of the Aboyne family, commonly called the Baron of Braikley. Invercy, who "came down Deeside whistlin an playin," was a relation of Gordon's, and of the name of Farquharson, a bold and darring freebooter in Braemar. The attack was made upon the Castle of Braikley by Invercy on the 16th of September, 1666, when John Gordon, his brother William, and several of his followers were killed.

There are various circumstances said to have given rise to this slaughter, but the most likely, in my opinion is, that it had been preconcerted between the baron's wife and Farquharson.

The Earl of Aboyne.

It is dangerous, at times, to jest with a female: for it is said that, where there is love, there is also jealousy.—A word in jest proved fatal in the present instance.

Bonny Peggy Irvine was, in my opinion, of the Irvines of Drum, one of the most ancient and honourable families in Aberdeenshire, whose ancestor, Alexander de Irvyne, was a son of Irvine of Bonshaw's, in the south of Scotland, who being armour-bearer to king Robert Bruce, had the lands and forest of Drum conferred upon him by that prince. The charter, still extant, is dated the eighteenth year of his reign, which fell in the year 1324. The king as a further mark of his favour gave Mr. Irvine for his armorial bearing three holly leaves, with a bundle of arrows for the crest, and the words *semper virens* for a motto ; which are said to have been the arms he himself bore when Earl of Carrick.

The Irvines of Drum have been connected with the principal families of Scotland, and renowned for their bravery, in the defence of the liberties of their country. One of the lairds of Drum, after he had slain Maclean, one of the highland chieftains, is thus respectfully mentioned in the old popular ballad of Harlaw.

>GUDE Sir Alexander Irving,
> The much renounit laird of Drum,
>Nane in his days were better sene,
> Quhen they were semblit all and sum.
>To praise him we sud not be dumm,
> For valor, wit and worthyness,
>To end his days he there did cumm,
> Quhois ransom is remeidyless.

Loch-in-var.

This copy, although far inferior in poetical merit to the one given in the Minstrelsy of the Scottish Border, under the title of " Katharine Janfarie," as it differs considerably in some of the particulars therein related, made me prefer it, being taken down from oral tradition.

Queen Eleanor's Confession.

Queen Eleanor was daughter and sole heiress of William duke of Guienne and Poictou, and had been married to Louis VII. sixteen years, at which period she attended him in a crusade to the Holy Land, but having lost the affection of her husband, and even fallen under some suspicions of gallantry with a handsome Saracen, Louis, more delicate than wise, procured a divorce from her, and restored her those rich provinces, which, by her marriage, she had annexed to the crown of France. Henry, then count of Anjou, though but in his nineteenth year, neither discouraged by the disparity of age, nor by the reports of Eleanor's gallantry, married her in six weeks after her divorce, and got possession of all her dominions as a dower. A marriage thus founded upon interest, was not likely to be very happy. Eleanor, who had disgusted her first husband by her gallantries, was no less offensive to her second by her jealousy; thus carrying to extremity in the different parts of her life, every circumstance of female weakness. She survived Henry many years, and died in 1204.

The Savage Blackamoor.

This is one of the most tragic ballads to be found in print. Its perusal is enough to chill the blood in the veins of the most hardened villain.

Lord Thomas and fair Eleanor.

The love of money is said to be the root of all evil: so it proved with Lord Thomas, fair Eleanor, and the brown girl.

Lady Anne.

Lady Anne seems to be almost a transcript from a very old ballad called The Minister's Daughter of New York, I lately took down from the singing of an old woman.

The Bonny Earl of Murray.

James VI. being jealous of an attachment betwixt his Queen, Anne of Denmark, and the Earl of Murray, the handsomest man of his time, prevailed with the deceitful Marquis of Huntly, his enemy, to murder him; and by a writing under his own hand, promised to save him harmless. He was killed at his castle of Dunibrissel on the 7th of January, 1592, with one of the Baskerville swords, which was lately in the possession of a dealer of curiosities in Edinburgh.—For the particulars of this murder, see Archbishop Spotwood's History of the Church of Scotland.

Clerk Colvill and the Mermaid.

The scene of this poem is laid at Slains, on the coast of Buchan, which is indented in many places by the sea with immense chasms, excavated in many places to a great extent. The author is said to be of the name of Clark, a drunken dominie in that parish, i. e. Slains, who was also author of a Poetical Dialogue between the Gardeners and the Tailors, on the origin of their crafts, and a most curious Latin and English poem called the Buttery College of Slains, which resembles much in language and stile, Drummond's (of Hawthornden) Polemo-Middinia.

Sir Patrick Spens.

This is one of the oldest ballads in the Scottish dialect, although history throws little light upon it. The scene of misfortune lies on the coast of Buchan, "half owre, half owre, to Aberdour," about twenty miles from Peterhead,

"And there lys gude Sir Patrick Spens,
Wi' the Scots lords at his feet."

There are various versions of this ancient ballad differing considerably from one another in the name and place. Some have the name Andrew Wood, and place Aberdeen.

Since this copy was printed, I have received from a very intelligent old man, four additional verses, which are as follows:

There shall no man go to my ship
 Till I say mass and dine;
And take my leave of my lady,
 Go to my bonny ship syne.

When he was up at the top-mast head,
 Around, could naething see;
But terrible storm in the air aboon,
 And below the roaring sea.

Come down, come down, my good master,
 You see not what I see;
For thro' an' thro' your bonny ship's side,
 I see the green salt sea.

Lang, lang will the ladies look,
 Wi' their gown-tails owre their crown,
Before they see Sir Patrick Spens
 Sailing to Dumferline town.

Andrew Lammie.

This is one of the greatest favourites of the people in Aberdeenshire that I know. I took it first down from the memory of a very old woman, and afterwards published thirty thousand copies of it. There are two versions, an old and a new; but, although I have both, I prefer this one, the younger of the two, having been composed and acted in the year 1674. The unfortunate maiden's name was Annie, or Agnes (which are synonymous in some parts of Scotland,) Smith, who died of a broken heart on the 9th January, 1631, as is to be found on a roughly cut stone, broken in many pieces, in the green church-yard of Fyvie.

Andrew Lammie, after learning the melancholy fate of his faithful Annie, returned immediately to Edinburgh, where, being in a public company, unknown to the audience, the song of his Annie, and their loves were sung and commented upon, when he was discovered by the buttons bursting off his waistcoat, and his falling down in a swoon. This will put many of my poetical readers in mind of the ballad of Lady Margerie, where it is said,—

But when brother Henry's cruel band
Had done the bloody deed,
The silver buttons flew off his coat,
And his nose began to bleed.

The Northern Lord and cruel Jew.

There is a ballad similar to this entitled "Gernutus the Jew of Venice;" but as this one is rarely to be met with, and possessing more incident, I prefer it.

The subject is taken from an Italian Novel, by Ser. Giovanni Fiorentino, who wrote in 1378. There is reason to believe that Shakespeare was indebted to the same work for his plot in the "Merchant of Venice."

Mary's Dream, (old way.)

The author of this exquisitely beautiful ballad is John Lowe, a native of Kenmore in Galloway. Mr. Lowe was originally a weaver, but by industry and close application to business, he soon earned as much, which with the assistance of friends, as enabled him to obtain a classical education at the University of Glasgow.—The loom being no ways calculated to call into action that genius which afterwards shone so conspicuously in Mary's Dream, and other of his lyric pieces. In 1773 he embarked for America, where he spent some time as a tutor to the family of a brother of the great Washington. He was soon after fortunate in obtaining a living in the Church of England, the then fashionable religion of the United States. Being united in the bands of wedlock to a Virginian lady of bad principles, he became melancholy, and, in the end dissipated, which brought him to an untimely grave in the forty eight year of his age.

He was born in the year 1750, and died at the house of a friend near Fredericksburgh, Virginia, in 1798, and now lies interred between two palm trees, with not a stone to mark the spot, nor whereon the passing spirit may write, 'Mary weep nae mair for me.'

Willie Wallace.

The copy of this ballad that is given here, was taken down from an itinerant tinker and gypsey, and it differs from every other that I have seen. The particulars related in it are to be found in blind Harry's metrical life of Sir William Wallace, the protector of his country, book fifth.

James Francis Edward Keith.

This ballad was written in honour of the above gentleman. who was born, according to the parish register, at Invernigic castle, St. Fergus, on the 16th June, 1696. At the age of 18, he went, at his mother's command, along with his brother, George earl Marischal, to the battle of Sherriff-muir, where his party were defeated, and he and his brother forced to flee to a foreign land to save their lives. In his state of exile, he entered the Spanish army, where he rose to the rank of a colonel. He afterwards served in the Russian and Prussian armies. He was killed at the head of his troops at the battle of Hochkirchen, in the service of the latter, in the year 1758, and 63d of his age. The king of Prussia caused him to be interred with military honours at Berlin, on the 3d of February, 1759.

Lorenzo.

It was a belief among the ancients, that there was such a charm in the plighted vows of lovers, that not even the dead could rest in their graves without the possession of the object of their affections.

> To me your vows you gave,
>   For you, false Rosa, have I died—
> To my dear mansion, the cold grave,
>   I come to bear away my bride!

The Death of Ella.

I may truly say with the pious Job, He (man) cometh forth like a flower, and is cut down; he fleeth also as a shadow, and continueth not. The apostle Peter also says, All flesh is grass, and the glory of man as the flower of grass. The grass withereth, and the flower therof falleth away. Even youth and beauty have not arts to deceive death and the grave!

Lord John.

In the ancient days of chivalry, it was common for the Scottish noblemen to visit the courts of foreign princes; sometimes in masquerade they woo'd the fair daughters of their hosts. Such was the conduct of Lord John,

> He's faen in love wi' the king's daughter,
> And to him she's with chile.

Lord Thomas of Winsberry.

This is a pear of the same tree.—The king of France daughter falls in love with Lord Thomas of Winsberry, who afterwards married her, and carried her to fair Scotland on a milk white steed, while he rode on a dapple grey.—Four wheeled carriages, in those days, were not the fashion.

Maria; or, the Maniac's Song.

This poem is original, and all those marked—B. are attempts by the Editor. This piece is founded on fact; and the poor young woman is to be daily seen a melancholy proof of what is therein related; but, since writing the above, I am happy to inform my readers that, through the humanity of some well-disposed persons, she is now carefully provided with a comfortable bed, provisions and clothes. She can give no account of herself whatever, and cannot, or will not even tell her name, nor whencesoever she came, she having appeared one day on the streets of Peterhead as if she had at that instant fallen from the clouds. It is conjectured by some, and even not at all improbable, that she might have been concerned in the new-year's day riot in Edinburgh, for which several unfortunate young men were executed; and, that love is the cause of her mourning.

Mary's Death—Summer, and Winter,

Were written on the impulse of the moment, and in the seasons to which they allude.

Beautiful Sue.

Was written out of respect to an amiable young woman in Edinburgh, who was afterwards married to an indulging young man, a Solicitor of the Supreme Courts, whose enjoyment was but of short duration. He, with four infant children, now mourn her premature death.

This song was the means of the author receiving a present of Fifty Pounds sterling.

May Morning — Roseate May — Cheerfu' Nancy — Edwin — Spotless Peggy and My Mary,

Were written during a fortnight's residence in Stirling

Love — Enjoyment — Generosity — Ingratitude — Poverty — The Complaint and The Storm,

May be called fragments, as they are incomplete of themselves, being disjoined from the prose to which they were originally attached—a biographical sketch of the author's life, drawn up at the request of the Right Hon. the Earl of Buchan, in the year 1819: but, as I never considered it of sufficient interest to attract public notice, it has lien by in the old portfolio ever since.

The Sherriff-muir Amazons.

Since this humorous ballad was printed, I have seen one similar to it called Paul Jones, but what claim it has to this title I know not, for it might, with equal propriety, be called the Apostle Paul, for it has no more connection with the one than the other. It chiefly refers to the French and the Spanish threatned invasion, with the changes that took place in Church and State in 1715, and the superstitions of the times.

My Mantle.

This Jacobite song was sung for many years in the neighbouring parishes of St. Fergus, Crimond, &c. as a New-year and Christmass pater, by a deputy of Homer's craft. It celebrates the landing of the Chevalier de St. George in Peterhead, on the 22nd of December, 1715, with some account of his reception there. I cannot say that it possesses much merit; but, as a local piece, I was fond of giving it a place, particularly, when every thing relative to the unfortunate House of Stuart is sought after with such avidity, and held in such estimation: and, to some of the Stuarts' votaries, what will no doubt be a strong recommendation is, that this note was written upon the indentical table at which JAMES VIII. eat his first diet of meat on his landing in Scotland, as it is now in the possession of the Editor.

Mossie and his Mare.

This is another of those satirical Jacobite songs that please and displease so much. There are various characters come in for their share of abuse; but I presume there have been many more in the original, but this is merely conjecture, as I could never find it, although I applied to upwards of fifty ballad and song-mongers, both old and young.

The Cadger's o' Whitcrook.

This is evidently one of the border ditties, which pleases me much; but I cannot say that every one will be of the same mind.—It appears to me to be very old. This copy was taken down from the singing of the Peterhead letter-carrier, who does it all manner of justice in the rehearsel or singing.

The Pipers o' Buchan.

Is the production of a tailor, who could not write a single letter, and one of the most eccentric characters of his time. It was my intention at first to have given some account of the author of this singular production, as I was intimately acquainted with him; but I have lately heard that his son, a veteran from the wars, intends publishing the whole poetical works, with a life of the old man, who died about eight years ago, which make me decline it.

Who would not admit that, this ballad in praise of our national music, should be Dedicated with all due respect to the Right Hon. the Earl of FIFE, the patron and friend of genius? Where is the Scotsman whose heart did not beat high, and his blood glow with pleasing emotion, on reading the animating speech of the noble President, at the last competition of Highland Pipers in Edinburgh?

As depicted in the ballad, our national music has charms in the hands of our brave countrymen, to cheer the wounded and dying hero. Out of hundreds of anecdotes that could be produced, I shall only give the following:—The Piper of the 71st regiment being severely wounded at the battle of Vimeira, in 1809, was unable to keep his legs, but this did not damp his military ardour, for raising himself on the ground he called out "I canna gang farther wi' you, lads, but deil hae' my saul if ye shall want music;" and he continued to animate them with his most warlike airs.

Lord and Lady Errol.

The hero of this strange piece was Gilbert Hay, who succeeded to the title of earl of Errol in the year 1636 He afterwards married Catherine, daughter of James, second earl of Southesk, but died without issue, anno 1674. The ballad is very old, and was popular among the vulgar in the north of Scotland. The curious but true circumstance which led to its composition is well known to many old people in this vicinity, and many lively anecdotes have been told concerning it. There are others on the same subject, to be met with in the south country, which differ materially from the present copy. In some of them it is said, that Kate Carnegy tries to poison her husband, a circumstance passed over in silence here. Thereis, however, enough of her good deeds shown.—She wished to divorse her husband for impotency, but failed in her shameful attempts; for after he had undergone the minutest scrutiny before the lords of Session, one of the ballads says, "And all the noblemen cried out that, Errol was a man." She was horribly enraged at this, denying it vehemently, adding, at the sametime, that——(Here I must let the curtain drop, I will not offend modesty; for Semiramis, queen of Egypt, would not have said more.)

Lord Salton and Auchanachie.

This is a fragment of which I can learn nothing.

Bonny John Seton.

This baron was a man of natural parts, improved with a liberal education and travelling. He was a steady loyalist, and while commanding a detachment of cavalry at the Bridge of Dee 1639, was shot through the heart in the 29th year of his age.

Mary Hamilton.

The present fragment differs considerably from the one given in the Minstrelsy of the Scottish Border.

The Burning of Frendraught House.

This ballad till now, was rarely to be met with, as it was thought by Mr. Ritson to have been lost. The particulars which led to the melancholy and diabolical act are as follows :—Upon the first of January 1630, the laird of Frendraught and his complices fell in a trouble with William Gordon of Rothiemay and his complices, where the said William was unhappily slain, being a gallant gentleman, and on Frendraught's side was slain George Gordon brother to James Gordon of Lesmoir, and divers others were hurt on both sides. The Marquis of Huntly, and some well-set friends settled this feud, and Frendraught ordained to pay to the lady relict of Rothiemay and the bairns, fifty thousand merks in composition of the slaughter, whilk as was said was truly paid.

Upon the 27th of September 1630, the laird of Frendraught having in his company Robert Creightoun of Caudlan, and James Lesly, son to John Lesly of Pitcaple, with some other servants, the said Robert after some speeches shoots the said James Lesly through the arm. They were parted, and he convoyed to Pitcaple, and the other Frendraught shot out of his company.

Likeas Frendraught upon the fifth of October held conference with the earl of Murray in Elgin, and upon the morn he came to the Bog of Gight, where the Marquis made him welcome. Pitcaple loups on about 30 horse in jack and spear, (hearing Frendraught's being in the Bog) upon Thursday the 7th October, and came to the marquis, who before his coming had discreetly directed Frendraught to confer with his lady. Pitcaple heavily complains of the hurt his son had got in Frendraught's company, and rashly avowed to be revenged before he went home. The marquis alledged Frendraught had done no wrong, and dissauded him from any trouble. Pitcaple, displeased with the marquis, suddenly went to horse, and that same day rides his own ways, leaving Frendraught behind him in the Bog, to whom the marquis revealed what conference was betwixt him and Pitcaple, and held him all that night and would not let him go. Upon the morn being Friday, and a night of October, the marquis caused Frendraught to breakfast lovingly and kindly; after breakfast, the marquis directs his dear son, viscount of Aboyne, with some servants to convoy Frendraught home to his own house, if Pitcaple was laid for him by the way: John Gordon, eldest son to the late slain Rothiemay happened to be in the Bog who would also go with Aboyne; they ride without interruption to the place of Frendraught, or sight of Pitcaple by the way. Aboyne took his leave from the laird, but upon no condition he and his lady would not suffer him to go, nor none that was with him that night, but earnestly urged him, (tho' against his will) to bide. They were well entertained, supped merrily, and went to bed joyfully. The viscount was laid in a bed in the old Tower going off the hall, and standing upon a vault, wherein there was an round hole devised of old, just under Aboyn's bed. Robert Gordon, born in Sutherland, his servitor, and English Will his page, were both laid beside him in the same chamber; the laird of Rothiemay with some servants beside him, was laid in an upper chamber just above Aboyn's; and in another room above that was laid George Chalmers of North and George Gordon another of the viscount's servants; with them also was laid captain Rollock, then in Frendraught's own company. Thus all being at rest, about midnight, that dolorous tower took fire in so sudden and furious manner that the viscount, the laird of Rothiemay, English Will, Colonel Ivat, another of Aboyn's servants, and other two, being six in number, were cruelly burnt and tormented to the death without help or relief. The laird of Frendraught, his lady and hail household, looking on, without moving or striving to deliver them from the fury of this fearful fire, as was reported. Robert Gordon, called Sutherland Robert, being in the viscount's chamber, escaped this fire with his life. George Chalmers and Captain Rollock, being in the third room, escaped also this fire, and as was said, Aboyn might have saved himself also, if he would have gone out of doors, which he would not do, but suddenly ran up stairs to Rothiemay's chamber and wakened him to rise; and as he is wakening him, the timber passage and lofting of the chamber hastily takes fire, so that none of them could win down stairs again, so they turned to a window looking to the close, where they piteously cryed many time, help, help! for God's cause! The laird and the lady with their servants all seeing the woeful crying, made no help nor manner of helping, which they perceiving, cried oftentimes mercy at God's hands for their sins, syne clasped in others arms, and cheerfully suffered their martyrdom. Thus died this noble viscount, of singular expectation, Rothiemay a brave youth, and the rest, by this doleful fire never enough to be deplored, to the great grief and sorrow of their kin, parents, and haill common people, especially to the marquis, who for his good will got this reward. No man can express the dolour of him and his lady, nor yet the grief of the visconut's own dear lady, when it came to her ears, which she kept to her dying day, disdaining after the company of man in her life time, following the love of the turtle dove.

(From an old author.)

Frennet Hall

Only recounts anew what is to be found in the preceding ballad of the Burning of Frendraught, an additional account of which catastrophe may be found in the 2nd vol. and 138 page of Gordon's History of the Gordons.

Lady Keith's Consolation.

This beautiful Jacobite melody is supposed to have been written by Lady Mary Drummond, daughter of the earl of Perth, and Countess of Marischall, during her stay at Inverugie Castle. Be this as it may, she is evidently, if not the author, the heroine of the piece.

Nae Dominies for me, Laddie.

The author of this excellent song was the Rev. John Forbes, minister at Deer, Aberdeenshire. This eccentric character was born at Pitnacalder, a small estate near Fraserburgh, of which his father was proprietor. From the name of his paternal spot, he was commonly designated Pitney, and better known by that appellation than that of his office. In his younger years, and before he was appointed encumbent at Deer, he wrote the well-known song of "Nae Dominies for me, Laddie," which seems to be a picture of himself, drawn from real life, and in which he took the greatest delight in singing and hearing sung. Even to his dying day did he persist in this whim, so much so, that, had he been going to the stake as a martyr, to expiate for unheard of crimes, in all probability, his dead-march would have been, "Nae Dominies for me, laddie." In the mean time may be inferred from the following four lines what his views were with regard to his future prospects.—

    But for your sake I'll fleece the flock,—
      Grow rich as I grow auld, lassie;
    If I be spar'd, I'll be a laird,
      And thou be madam call'd, lassie.

In the latter part of his life, he was not so happy in his poetical compositions, as we may judge from a collection of Spiritual Songs, published by him in 1757.

In the end of this collection, there is a curious dissertation, "Wherein the late Innovation in Church Music is particularly considered." He was a rigid Presbyterian, and said by some to possess the gift of prophecy. Many curious anecdotes are told of him. He died in 1769, and was buried in the church-yard of Old Deer, where a plain stone is placed to his memory, bearing the following appropriate inscription:—" Dedicated by Mrs. Margaret Hay, widow, to the memory of John Forbes of Pitnacalder, M. A Minister of Deer, who died anno 1769 in the 81st year of his age, and the 52nd of his ministry. With a manly figure, he possessed the literature of the Scholar, the elocution of the Preacher, and the accomplishment of the Gentleman. As a Pastor, his character was distinguished by piety, virtue, and entire devotion to the cause of Christ. Beloved by his relatives, respected by his acquaintances, venerated by the body of his people; his life was useful, and his end was peace.

Logie o' Buchan.

The author of this song, George Halket, was born in Aberdeenshire, but in what place, or in what year is not certain; he was, however, parochial schoolmaster at Rathen, in the years 1736 and 7. He inherited a rich vein of humour for satirical poetry, which was dedicated, like most of his cotemporaries to the service or aggrandizement of the Jacobite party. His poetry was long familiar to the peasants in that corner of the country, and rehearsed and sung by them at their festivals and merry mettings with great eclat, some of them having a religious tendancy.

He is the author of the well-known Jacobite song of " Whirry Whigs awa man,"although he contrived to fath er it upon a

"————————————Will Jack,
Who had Corskelly boats in tack,
But who could neither read nor write,
Tho' wonderfully could indite."

Which are the lines commonly appended to most copies of this song, and which have led people to think this William Jack was the author. From Rathen, he was obliged to remove to the fishing town of Cairnbulg, for having a scuffle with Mr. Anderson, (who was at that time minister,) in the church upon a sunday. He continued long in Cairnbulg, and had a full school. It was here where Whirry Whigs was written. In the year 1750 he removed to Memsie, where he taught the late colonel Fraser of that place, and sir James Innes' children, who were at that time residing at Tyrie, the principal part of their education, for which he received six bolls of meal and three bolls of malt per year, besides his liberty to teach as many more as he pleased, whose fees amounted to a considerabl sum, having upward of seventy. He had two wives, the first was smothered in the snow between Fraserburgh and her own house, on her way home from the former, and left no children. The second had three sons and one daughter; one of the sons was a writer to his Majesty's Signet, Edinburgh; another was captain of a ship, and the third was an assistant to his father till he died—the son afterwards went to the West Indies.

Mr. Halket wrote a great many poems, several of which are in my possession, altho' most of them were suppressed as soon as they made their appearance, as he sent them orphans into the world: for him, at that time, to have done otherwise, would have been dangerous. Indeed, such was the loyalists' rage against him, that, for one of his little pieces, written in the beginning of 1746, (A Dialogue between the Devil and George II.) he had a hair-breadth-scape, a copy of it having fallen into the duke of Cumberland's hands when he was in Banff, on his way to Culloden. A reward of £100 being offered by him for its author, either dead or alive. I am sorry it is not in my power to indulge the inquisitive reader with a perusal of this so obnoxious ballad, as now no trace of it can be found, as it had, in all probability, been crushed in embryo, upon the duke's threatened anathema. He wrote also "Schism Displayed, in its various colours and confusions," which was printed at Oxford, according to the fashion of the times, in a six column ballad, embellished with a large tree in the centre, and the word Presbytric at the root, with the names of the different sects which had sprung from it, attached to their respective branches. At the foot of the tree there was a devil with a hou cleaning the ground from its root; at each side there are two other devils prooning the branches. On the left hand side stood

Oliver Cromwell, with these words above him, "Oliver Cromwell, chief head of the fanaticks, pontive of hell." To him the devil addresses the following apostrophe :—

"Behold the man, who by vile faction taught,
On England's church and state destruction brought:
Behold the hypocrite, who dared employ
Religion's cloak, religion to destroy.
Behold the devil, who with Jewish pride,
Martyr'd his king, and heaven and laws defied;
A king to whom the Graces all combin'd,
In wisdom, virtue, and a God-like mind!"

Like his cotemporary Meston, Halkit shared the taciturnity of fortune in retreat, for he was obliged to leave the fruitful fields and sunny knows of Memsie, and for some time had no where to lay his head. After a considerable lapse of time, he again settled as a private teacher at Tyrie, but whether he had ere this time sung his requiem to the muses, and bidden them a final adieu, I cannot, with certainty say, but I hear no more of him bestriding Pegasus.

The charming little song of "Logie o' Buchan," was written while Mr. Halkit was at Rathen. The Logie mentioned in the song is in one of the adjoining parishes, (Crimond,) where Mr. Halkit resided; and the Jamie "that delv'd in the yard," the hero of the piece, was a James Robertson, gardener at the place of Logie, and who "played on the pipe and the viol sae sma." A son of Jamie's is still alive, a very old man, to whom I wrote in hopes of obtaining more information anent the author; but his ignorance, indolance, or both, has as yet prevented him sending me any answer. But Mr. R's negligence is perhaps owing to his not wishing the world to know his father's weaknesses, and that he is one of the living memorials of Jamie's illicit amours.

The original Logie o' Buchan begins thus:—

O woe to Kinmundy, Kinmundy the laird,
Wha's taen awa Jamie that delv'd in the yard,
Wha play'd on the pipe and the viol sae sma,
Kinmundy's taen Jamie the flower o' them a'.

Mr. Halkit died where he had spent the most pleasant part of his life at Memsie, in the year 1756, and was buried within the old church-yard of Fraserburgh, at the west end of the aisle.

By the side of a Country kirk wall.

This song was written by the late Rev. John Skinner, Longside, near Peterhead. The "sullen Whig minister" here alluded to, was the Rev John Forbes, minister of Deer, and author of "Nae Dominies for me, laddie." As I have already given some account of Mr. Forbes, I shall only advert a little to that of Mr. Skinner's—He was a poet superior to most of his cotemporaries, and the friend of Burns. Many of his pieces never were published, but handed about in MS. as they were local, and only applied to events which had at that time taken place in his neighbourhood. He was agreeable and facinating in company, and esteemed by all ranks of his congregation. His writings in general, are severe and caustic as the present song will testify. On the 16th of June 1807, in the arms of his son, the Right Rev John Skinner, he slept the sleep of death, and was buried in the church-yard of Longside, aged 86.

Charly now that's o'er the sea.

In my zeal for Mr. Hogg's cause, when collecting the Jacobite Relics of Scotland, I could not withstand the temptation one drowsy night of making one solitary attempt myself, and lo, here it is!

Adam o' Gordon.

Both Buchanan, Spotswood, and Gordon, mention this inhuman affair of sir Adam Gordon of Auchindown, and brother to the marquis of Huntly. Sir Adam Gordon was an active partizan for Queen Mary, under the shadow of whose authority he committed divers oppressions, especially upon the Forbeses. In 1571, he sent one captain Ker with a party on foot to summon the castle of Towie in the queen's name. The Alexander Forbes was not at home, and his lady confiding too much in her sex. not only refused to surrender, but gave Ker very injurious language; upon which, unreasonably transported with fury, he ordered his men to set fire to the castle, and barbarously burnt the unfortunate gentlewoman, great with child, her children, and whole family, amounting to thirty-seven persons. Nor was he ever so much as cashiered for this inhuman action.

F I N I S.

www.ingramcontent.com/pod-product-compliance
Lightning Source LLC
Chambersburg PA
CBHW031824230426
43669CB00009B/1221